Book One

All Together
SUNDAY SCHOOL

When You Have Kids of All Ages in One Room

Group

R·E·A·L
RELATIONAL EXPERIENTIAL APPLICABLE LIFELONG

Group resources really work!

This Group resource incorporates our R.E.A.L. approach to ministry. It reinforces a growing friendship with Jesus, encourages long-term learning, and results in life transformation, because it's:

Relational
Person-to-person interaction enhances spiritual growth and builds Christian friendships.

Experiential
What we experience through action and discussion sticks with us up to 9 times longer than what we simply hear or read.

Applicable
The aim of ministry is to equip people to be both hearers and doers of God's Word.

Lifelong
Experiences transform the heart, moving faith beyond the walls of church and into everyday life for years to come.

All Together Sunday School
Book One

Copyright © 2024 Group Publishing, Inc./0000 0001 0362 4853

All rights reserved. No part of this book may be reproduced in any manner whatsoever without prior written permission from the publisher, except where noted in the text and in the case of brief quotations embodied in critical articles and reviews. For information, visit group.com/permissions.

Visit our website: group.com

Credits

Art Director: Jeff Storm

Illustrator: Carolyn Williams

Chief Creative Officer: Joani Schultz

Executive Director of Content Creation: Jody Brolsma

Executive Editor: Charity Kauffman

Copy Editor: Lyndsay Gerwing

Contributing Editor: Laycie McClain

Scripture quotations are taken from the *Holy Bible*, New Living Translation, copyright © 1996, 2004, 2015 by Tyndale House Foundation. Used by permission of Tyndale House Publishers, Inc., Carol Stream, Illinois 60188. All rights reserved.

ISBN 978-1-4707-7614-5

Printed in the U.S.A.

10 9 8 7 6 5 4 3 2 1   27 26 25 24

Group

Table of Contents

Welcome to All Together Sunday School 4

All Together Tasks Labels 8

Feelings Chart 9

1 **God Creates** 10
  Discover Genesis 1:1

2 **God Is Most Important** 22
  Discover Exodus 20:3

3 **God Sees Our Hearts** 34
  Discover 1 Samuel 16:7

4 **God Takes Care of Us** 46
  Discover Psalm 23:1

5 **God Is in Charge** 58
  Discover Psalm 46:10

6 **God Gives Us Hope** 70
  Discover Jeremiah 29:11

7 **Jesus Cares** 82
  Discover Matthew 11:28

8 **Jesus Loves Children** 94
  Discover Mark 10:14

9 **Jesus Brings Joy** *Works for Christmas!* 106
  Discover Luke 2:10-11

10 **Jesus Shows Us How to Love** 118
  Discover John 13:34

11 **The Holy Spirit Gives Us Power** 130
  Discover Acts 1:8

12 **Jesus Saves Us** *Works for Easter!* 142
  Discover Romans 10:9

13 **God's Love Never Stops** 154
  Discover 1 Corinthians 13:7

Download a Digital Copy!

The All Together Sunday School Digital Download Center contains digital versions of this book and its handouts. Use your unique access code to log on, then find what you need!

Welcome to All Together Sunday School

All Together Sunday School gives you a fresh way to help kids of all ages hear from God through his Word. In each lesson, kids explore one key Bible verse—as they play!

At your church, are combined-age groups a must-do or a choose-to?

Let's face it, sometimes combining kids of different ages at church feels like a must-do instead of a choose-to.

But combined-age groups *can* be a choose-to, too! As we designed All Together Sunday School, we discovered an upside to mixing things up. Combined-age classrooms are a strategic choice for your church family because they help you more effectively guide kids to grow in relationship with Jesus and each other.

In developing All Together Sunday School, we observed multi-age kids in their natural habitats—the playground, the living room, the church picnic—then we tailored Bible lessons to the natural rhythms of play and relationship-growing we observed. This fresh approach to Bible teaching combines discipleship and play for kids of all ages. Trust us, you *and* the kids you lead are gonna love it!

These Bible lessons, geared for ages 4-12, work any time you have kids of all ages in one room. Need lessons for Sunday school, children's church, midweek programs, moms' groups? We have you covered! Lessons are designed to last about an hour—with built-in flexibility to work for more or less time as needed.

Here's our not-so-secret recipe. It's how All Together Sunday School helps you effectively prepare meaningful Bible discoveries for combined-age groups.

Step 1

All Together Sunday School lessons help you prepare your environment *and* kids' hearts.

All Together Sunday School creates an environment that kids of all ages actually *want* to be in. Environment is more than the room in which you meet; it's the atmosphere—the vibe! It's the spirit leaders cultivate and the Holy Spirit creates.

Meaningful Bible experiences empower kids with responsibility and choice. That's why kids choose jobs at the beginning of each All Together Sunday School lesson. As we tested these experiences, we found that responsibility grows relationships. Kids encourage each other in their roles, form friendships, and love being in charge sometimes, too. Here are the tasks kids choose from each week. (See page 8.)

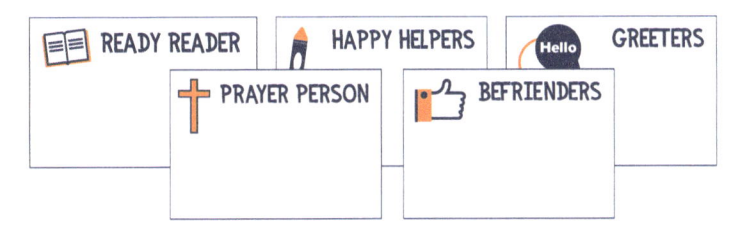

Talk Together

All Together Sunday School also creates an environment where kids can develop social and emotional skills. The Talk Together section is a powerful and intentional way for you to form friendships with kids and for kids to better befriend each other. Each week, kids communicate how their day is going, with the help of a fun and user-friendly Feelings Chart. (See page 9.)

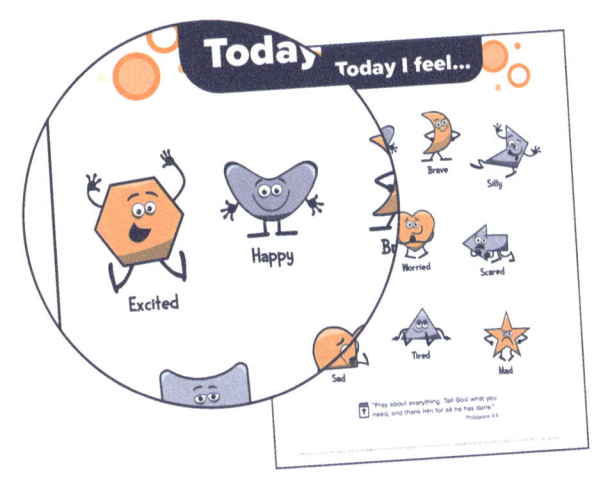

Pray Together

After they talk about how they're feeling, your group will Pray Together and tell God about what's going on in their minds and their hearts.

This powerful prayer time:

- Builds trust and relationships in your combined-age group.
- Provides an opportunity for kids to pray and talk with God about what's going on in their lives.
- Prepares kids' hearts to hear what God has to say back to them through the Bible verse they'll explore all together.

Step 2

> All Together Sunday School lessons help you disciple through play.

Each child brings his or her own unique personality and age-specific needs to your classroom. All Together Sunday School creates meaningful Bible experiences that attend to each child's needs.

Play Together

Hear this: Discipleship through play is not a free-for-all. Rather, it's inviting kids to choose purposeful play that helps them connect Bible truth to fun experiences. These fun-filled Bible lessons always integrate toys in order to bring kids together and teach Bible truth. In order to prepare for each lesson, you'll place specific items in the Wonder What Bin!

The Wonder What Bin is a key part of each All Together Sunday School lesson. This large container will store the toys and supplies needed for "Play Together" and "Wonder What Stations." Each week, kids will "wonder what" is in store for them! Your Wonder What Bin could be a plastic storage bin, a treasure chest, a toy box, or any large container.

Each All Together Sunday School lesson begins and ends with play.

- The **Play Together** section presents two options to begin your class time. Each activity takes about five minutes and invites kids to enter the space, get to know each other, and find out what Bible verse they'll explore that day.

READ	GAMES	IMAGINE THAT	OBJECT LESSON	CRAFT
Take a Look	Let's Play	Imaginative Play	Try This	Create

- **Wonder What Stations** are free-flowing application activities for after the Bible Discovery. Each lesson includes three of these five types of activities. No matter what kids' interests and learning preferences, there is something for everyone! Kids enjoy these application activities for 15-20 minutes, depending on the amount of time you have together.

Step 3

> All Together Sunday School helps you cover *less* Bible content *more* deeply by studying key Bible verses in context.

All Together Sunday School focuses on Bible truth, not just Bible knowledge. As you serve up Bible truth, All Together Sunday School starts small—with one beloved Bible verse per lesson. We created the scope and sequence by asking children's ministry leaders what verses they most want to teach kids. Check them out—they create a solid foundation for Bible learning.

Bible Discovery

The Bible Discovery section of each All Together Sunday School lesson helps kids place the Bible verse in the big story of Scripture. Each Bible Discovery takes about 15 minutes and is packed with action and experiences that engage kids of all ages—even the little ones! Exploring key verses in context naturally leads to deep Bible learning for everyone.

Here & Home Papers

Even after the lesson concludes, the fun continues! Kids work on a cool, interactive coloring activity page as they wait for their grown-ups to pick them up after class. Flip over the page, and find fun activities for families to do as they continue to explore and apply the Bible verse at home.

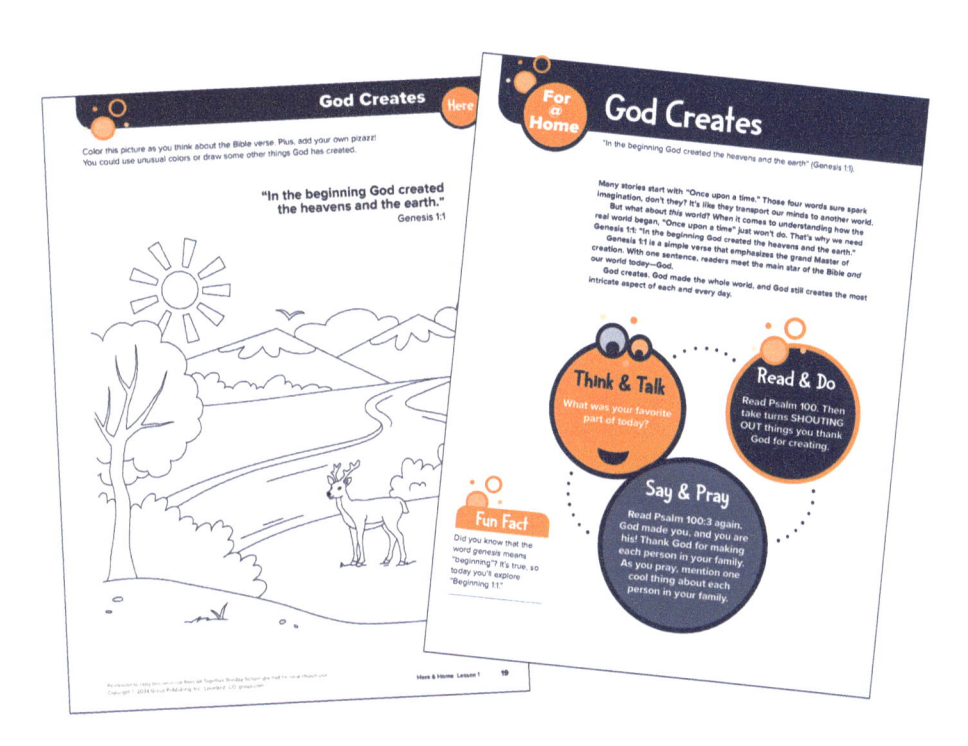

📖 **READY READER**	✝ **PRAYER PERSON**
🖍 **HAPPY HELPER**	🖍 **HAPPY HELPER**
👍 **BEFRIENDER**	👍 **BEFRIENDER**
💬 Hello **GREETER**	💬 Hello **GREETER**

Permission to copy this resource from All Together Sunday School granted for local church use. Copyright © 2024 Group Publishing, Inc., Loveland, CO. group.com

Today I feel...

- Excited
- Happy
- Brave
- Silly
- Peaceful
- Worried
- Scared
- Sad
- Tired
- Mad

"Pray about everything. Tell God what you need, and thank him for all he has done."
Philippians 4:6

Lesson 1: God Creates

"In the beginning God created the heavens and the earth" (Genesis 1:1).

Discover Genesis 1:1

Many stories start with "Once upon a time." Those four words sure spark imagination, don't they? It's like they transport our minds to another world.

But what about *this* world? When it comes to understanding how the real world began, "Once upon a time" just won't do. That's why we need Genesis 1:1: "In the beginning God created the heavens and the earth."

Genesis 1:1 is a simple verse that emphasizes the grand Master of creation. With one sentence, readers meet the main star of the Bible *and* our world today—God.

God creates. God made the whole world, and God still creates the most intricate aspect of each and every day—and this lesson.

- God's creating a place in kids' hearts to receive and understand this cosmic verse.
- God's creating ideas in *your* mind for how to lead this lesson well.
- God's creating personalities and possibilities for all the children in your class, no matter how old they are.

God creates. So let's trust that, through your time together, God will create friendships, discovery, and aha moments where kids realize what a wonderful world ours really is and what a wonderful Creator we truly have.

PRAYER

Oh God, create in me a loving heart and a wise mind, that I may respond to your children with grace and truth today. In Jesus' name, amen.

Fun Fact

Did you know that the word *genesis* means "beginning"? It's true, so today you'll explore "Beginning 1:1."

Lesson Overview

Bible Verse: Genesis 1:1 | **Bible Point:** God creates. *(It's true!)* | **Bible Exploration:** Genesis 1:1–2:3

Lesson-at-a-Glance

Play Together (10-15 minutes)
Make up a new game with items in the Wonder What Bin and/or play Creation I Spy.

Talk Together | Pray Together (10 minutes)
Talk about how you're feeling today, then pray and talk with God about it.

Bible Discovery (10-15 minutes)
Find and read Genesis 1:1 together, design a Creation mural, and talk about what makes God special.

Wonder What Stations (15-20 minutes)
Choose and move through the following activities:
- Take a Look: Look at nature books.
- Let's Play: Put a puzzle together.
- Imagine That: Play with animal figurines, creating different scenes and stories for the animals.

Review Together (5 minutes)
Explore a Jesus Connection, work together to create actions for words in the Bible Verse, and give out Here & Home papers.

Supply List

- ☐ Bible bookmarked at Genesis 1:1
- ☐ All Together Tasks labels (1 sheet for every 8 kids) (on page 8)
- ☐ Feelings Charts (1 for every 2 kids) (on page 9)
- ☐ large pieces of bulletin board paper (1 for every 3-5 kids)
- ☐ painter's tape
- ☐ crayons
- ☐ glue sticks
- ☐ brown construction paper (3 pieces for every 3-5 kids)
- ☐ Here & Home papers (1 per child) (on page 19)

Wonder What Bin Contents

- ☐ playground balls
- ☐ jump-ropes
- ☐ toy animal figurines
- ☐ puzzles
- ☐ books and magazines about nature

The "Wonder What Bin"

This supply box is a key part of each All Together Sunday School lesson. It will store all the toys and supplies needed for the Play Together activities and Wonder What Stations. Each week, kids will "wonder what" is in store for them! Your Wonder What Bin could be a storage bin, a toy box, or any large container.

Lesson 1

All Together Tasks

Supplies: All Together Tasks labels (1 sheet for every 8 kids)

As kids arrive, explain the special jobs and encourage each child to choose one to do today. Download and print the All Together Tasks labels or copy them from page 8, and let kids choose the jobs they want to do. It's okay if more than one child has the same job or if one child has a few jobs. Teachers can have another job, too!

Kids choose from the following jobs:

Ready Reader is ready and willing to read a Bible verse aloud.

Prayer Person prays aloud nice and loud so everyone can hear.

Happy Helpers jump at the chance to hand out supplies and clean up stuff.

Befrienders are on the lookout for those who need help and support.

Greeters say, "Hello and welcome!" to everyone as they arrive and "Have a good day!" to everyone as they leave.

Play Together (10-15 minutes)

Play with the kids, using their favorite toys and games to help introduce the Bible Point. Choose one or both activities.

Create-a-Game

Supplies:
- Wonder What Bin

Work together or with a friend or two to make up a new game! Using the supplies in the Wonder What Bin, create games to play together. For example, you could hide animal figurines and have friends find them, or you could try to roll a ball into a jump-rope circle.

Ask: What was it like to create something new?

Say: Today we'll explore a Bible verse that tells us who created the whole world. Spoiler alert: It was God! God is good at making new things because <u>God creates</u>.

Creation I Spy

Play Creation I Spy. Go outside or gather by a window or two. One person goes first, choosing something seen in nature and saying, "I spy with my little eye something God made that's [color]." Kids take turns guessing what was seen. Whoever guesses correctly goes next.

Say: <u>God creates</u>! Cool things we see outside don't just magically appear. From itty-bitty bugs to fancy feathers to mighty mountains, God is the Creator of everything! God still creates the cool things in nature we see today.

Ask: What's a cool plant, bug, or animal you've seen?

Ask: What does that cool thing tell you about God?

12   All Together Sunday School Book 1

Talk Together (5 minutes)

Kids talk in pairs about how they're feeling today.

Say: Today we'll talk with God and hear what God has to say to us through words in the Bible. But first, let's talk together. How are you feeling today?

Form pairs, and give each pair a Feelings Chart and a crayon. Have partners each circle the face that reflects how they're feeling in this moment and then tell their partners why they chose that face. Be sure to find a partner, too, and participate with the kids as they chat.

Pray Together (5 minutes)

Kids tell God how they're feeling and pray a prayer all together.

Say: Thanks for talking with a friend! In the Bible, we read that we can pray and tell God anything. You'll see the words of that Bible verse printed on the Feelings Chart. If you'd like to read along, please do! Or just listen as I read God's words.

Philippians 4:6 says, "Pray about everything. Tell God what you need, and thank him for all he has done."

Like we just talked with our friends, we can talk with God! Let's practice doing that now! We'll silently pray and tell God how we're feeling today. We won't pray with our voices—instead we'll just think a prayer to God for a little bit. After our thinking prayer, we'll pray a special prayer all together.

Invite kids to get comfortable and close their eyes as they pray.

Pray: Dear God, we want to tell you how we feel today and why we feel that way. Pause for several moments of silent prayer. Thanks for listening, God.

Say: Now let's pray all together. We'll ask God to guide our time together today. Watch and do what I do! After each sentence, I'll pause and we'll say the words "All together" together!

Pray: Dear God,

    May we love [make the shape of a heart with your hands] **you and each other.** ("All together!")

    May we listen [cup hand behind ear] **to you and each other.** ("All together!")

    May we learn [point to brain] **about you and each other.** ("All together!")

    May we laugh and have fun [high-five a friend] **with you and each other.** ("All together!")

    Thanks for bringing us ("All together!") **today. Amen.**

Supplies:
- Feelings Charts (1 for every 2 kids)
- crayons

Download and print or make one copy of the Feelings Chart on page 9 for every two people. Instead of printing each week, consider placing the charts in plastic sheet protectors. Then kids can use dry-erase markers to mark how they're feeling. Simply clean off the markings for next week!

This prayer will set the tone for your time together each lesson. Each sentence helps to communicate the values in your classroom and invites God to help everyone do their part, no matter their age! When behavior challenges arise, you can guide kids back to this prayer, to steer them toward loving behaviors.

📖 Bible Discovery (15 minutes)

Find and read a verse together, explore its Bible context, and talk about stories in the Bible that reinforce the main idea of the verse.

Supplies:
- Bible bookmarked at Genesis 1:1
- large pieces of bulletin board paper (1 for every 3-5 kids)
- painter's tape
- crayons
- glue sticks
- brown construction paper (3 pieces for every 3-5 kids)

Find and read Genesis 1:1.

Beforehand, use painter's tape to attach a large piece of bulletin board paper to a wall. Prepare 1 piece for every 3-5 kids.

Say: Let's hear a Bible verse that'll help us get to know God even better. Today we'll explore Genesis 1:1.

The Bible is made up of Bible *books, chapters,* and *verses*. Chapters are longer and verses are shorter—usually about one sentence.

Let's hear Genesis 1:1. It's the very first verse in the Bible! Genesis is the book, the first "1" is the chapter, and the second "1" is the verse.

Invite the Ready Reader to read the verse from your marked Bible. Have everyone clap to thank the Ready Reader for reading.

Ask: What does this verse tell us about God?

Say: This verse tells us that God creates! That's our Bible Point today. So every time you hear the words "God creates," give two thumbs up and say, "It's true!" To practice, repeat the Bible Point and response several times.

The world began when God created it. Listen while I read Genesis 1:1 again. Read the verse from a Bible again.

When we say the word "beginning," we're talking about how something started. Our world had a beginning. And your day today had a beginning, too!

Ask: What did you do to begin your day today? Invite responses from the whole group.

Say: You began your day by getting dressed, eating breakfast, and brushing your teeth. Genesis 1:1 tells us how the world started. The world didn't start on its own—God started it! "In the beginning, God created the heavens and the earth." God creates. *(It's true!)*

When we keep reading Genesis chapter 1, we find out more about the world God created. God created a whole bunch of stuff!

Design a creation mural.

Let's create our own little world while we discover what God created. We'll use our imaginations a bit and make a Creation mural! A mural is a really big picture.

Motion to the large piece of bulletin board paper. Have the Happy Helpers distribute crayons, glue sticks, and construction paper.

14 All Together Sunday School Book 1

Let's begin, artists! First God created light. Then God created water and sky. Choose a child to draw wavy lines at the bottom of the mural and a child to color the top of the mural blue.

God created land and seas. Choose a child to glue brown construction paper to make land across the middle of the mural. Invite other kids to scribble blue seas all around the land.

And God created plants and trees. Have kids draw plants and trees on the land.

God created the sun and the moon. Choose a child to draw the sun at the top of one side of the mural and a moon at the top of the other side.

God saw that what he made was good. And I think our mural looks pretty good, too. Thanks for helping create it. Now our bodies will become part of the picture too! I'll show you what I mean. Let's be creative and use our imaginations for this next part.

God created fish and birds. Call out different fish and birds for kids to act out. Ideas include sharks, whales, octopuses, starfish, dolphins, penguins, chickens, eagles, and hummingbirds. Invite kids to call out different fish and birds to act out in front of the mural, too.

God created big animals and small animals. Have kids stand in front of the mural again, and call out big and small animals, alternating big and small. Ideas include spiders, bears, mice, lions, porcupines, and elephants.

And last, and most important of all, God created people. God made a man named Adam and a woman named Eve. Choose a child to draw two stick figures on the construction paper "land."

People are God's most special creations. Listen to this!

Read aloud Genesis 1:27.

<u>God creates</u>. *(It's true!)* **We can be sure that nothing in our world just appeared on its own. God created it! And God's most special creations are people—including you and me!** Have kids turn to each other and say, "It's true! God created you."

Talk about God, the Creator.

Have kids look at their mural creations to review things God created. Compliment their creations.

Ask: What's something God created that you really like?

Ask: How was creating this mural different from how God created the whole world?

Say: We needed supplies and directions. But God didn't. God is the Creator. God spoke, and things were made. And those things were good! The words in the Bible tell us what God thought about the things he made. Listen to this!

Read aloud Genesis 1:31.

Show the book of Genesis in a Bible. **At the time these words were written in the Bible, people had all kinds of ideas about how the world began. Some people thought angry gods were fighting and their fights started the world. Made-up creation stories talk about fake gods who fight. But the one true God is different. <u>God creates</u>.** *(It's true!)*

Made-up creation stories talk about gods not caring about people. But not our God! **God loves the people <u>God creates</u>.** *(It's true!)*

Even today we may read or hear other stories about how the world began. **But Genesis 1 tells us the truth about who's really been in charge since the beginning—God! Remember, "in the beginning, God created the heavens and the earth." <u>God creates</u>.** *(It's true!)*

Pray together.

Sit together in a circle. **Let's talk to God again and thank God for creating. We'll go around the circle and call out things God made. Let's go around a few times. I'll thank God for a certain kind of thing he made. Then we'll go around the circle and each say something in that category.**

Prayer Person, will you talk with God for us to end the prayer? I'll give you a signal when it's time.

Pray: Dear God, we thank you for the world you've created. And we thank you that you still make things new each and every day.

We thank you, God, for creating bugs like…

We thank you, God, for creating plants like…

We thank you, God, for creating fish like…

We thank you, God, for creating big animals like…

We thank you, God, for creating small animals like…

We thank you, God, for creating family members like…

We thank you, God, for creating friends like…

We thank you, God, for creating everyone and everything.

Amen.

Wonder What Stations (15-20 minutes)

> Kids will wonder and wander their way through these three free-flowing application activities. Young kids may gravitate toward some things while older kids are drawn to others.

Say: Let's keep exploring Genesis 1:1 with the items in this Wonder What Bin. You'll have three choices—I wonder what you'll choose to do first!

Dramatically re-reveal what's inside the Wonder What Bin, and explain these three different options for kids to choose during a free-play time. After 15-20 minutes, tell kids you'll be cleaning up the Wonder What Stations in about a minute. Have Happy Helpers return supplies to the Wonder What Bin.

Supplies:
- Wonder What Bin

Take a Look

Look through books and magazines or ask an adult to do a search on a smartphone for interesting facts about God's creation.

Ask: Think about all the cool stuff God created. What do the things God created tell us about God?

Say: God's creation shows how smart God is. And how much God likes things to be in order. And how God pays attention to the teeny-tiniest things. And how big and strong God is! In the beginning, God created the heavens and the earth. <u>God creates</u>. *(It's true!)*

Let's Play

Put a puzzle together! Then look at the completed picture. What do you see that God created?

Say: Each piece of this puzzle fits together in a special way. Like we created a beautiful picture with these puzzle pieces, <u>God creates</u>. *(It's true!)*

God is creating beautiful things in the world today!

Ask: What are some beautiful things you notice God creating in our world now?

As kids play, meander around the area, using these questions and comments to connect each activity to today's Bible verse and Bible Point.

Imagine That

Play with animal figurines, creating different scenes and stories for the animals.

Say: How fun! Our creative God made you so creative, too! Even right now, <u>God creates</u> cool things through you! *(It's true!)* **And I'm so glad I got to see it.**

Ask: What are some cool things God has inspired people to create?

Lesson 1

Review Together (5 minutes)

> Explore a Jesus Connection and work together to create actions for words in the Bible verse.

Supplies:
- Here & Home papers (1 per child)
- crayons

Say: God created in the beginning. And God has been creating and putting things in order ever since. God is creating right now!

Let's create some actions to do as we say Genesis 1:1 all together. Rather than *me* telling you what to do, you kids can create the actions for us. You're in charge!

Invite kids to work together to make up actions for these words:

- beginning
- God
- created

Say Genesis 1:1 together with actions:
"In the beginning, God created the heavens and the earth."

People didn't create the heavens and the earth. Monsters didn't create the heavens and the earth. God did! God is in charge of everything in the whole world because God made it all.

God loved people so much that he would one day send his Son, Jesus, to live on earth to show God's love in a big and surprising way.

God creates. *(It's true!)* And God created you in a super-special way. When you create, you're showing off the amazing way God made you!

Take some time to affirm kids by name, mentioning something cool about the way God created each of them.

Here & Home

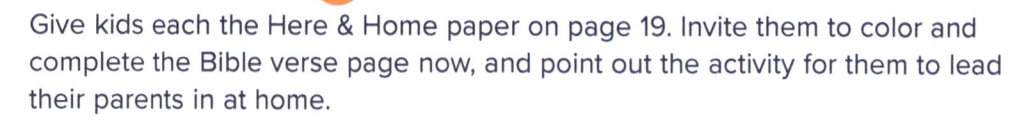

Give kids each the Here & Home paper on page 19. Invite them to color and complete the Bible verse page now, and point out the activity for them to lead their parents in at home.

God Creates

Color this picture as you think about the Bible verse. Plus, add your own pizazz! You could use unusual colors or draw some other things God has created.

"In the beginning God created the heavens and the earth."

Genesis 1:1

Here & Home Lesson 1

Home

God Creates

"In the beginning God created the heavens and the earth" (Genesis 1:1).

Many stories start with "Once upon a time." Those four words sure spark imagination, don't they? It's like they transport our minds to another world.

But what about *this* world? When it comes to understanding how the real world began, "Once upon a time" just won't do. That's why we need Genesis 1:1: "In the beginning God created the heavens and the earth."

Genesis 1:1 is a simple verse that emphasizes the grand Master of creation. With one sentence, readers meet the main star of the Bible *and* our world today—God.

God creates. God made the whole world, and God still creates the most intricate aspect of each and every day.

Fun Fact

Did you know that the word *genesis* means "beginning"? It's true, so today you'll explore "Beginning 1:1."

Think & Talk

What was your favorite part of today?

Read & Do

Read Psalm 100. Then take turns SHOUTING OUT things you thank God for creating.

Say & Pray

Read Psalm 100:3 again. God made you, and you are his! Thank God for making each person in your family. As you pray, mention one cool thing about each person in your family.

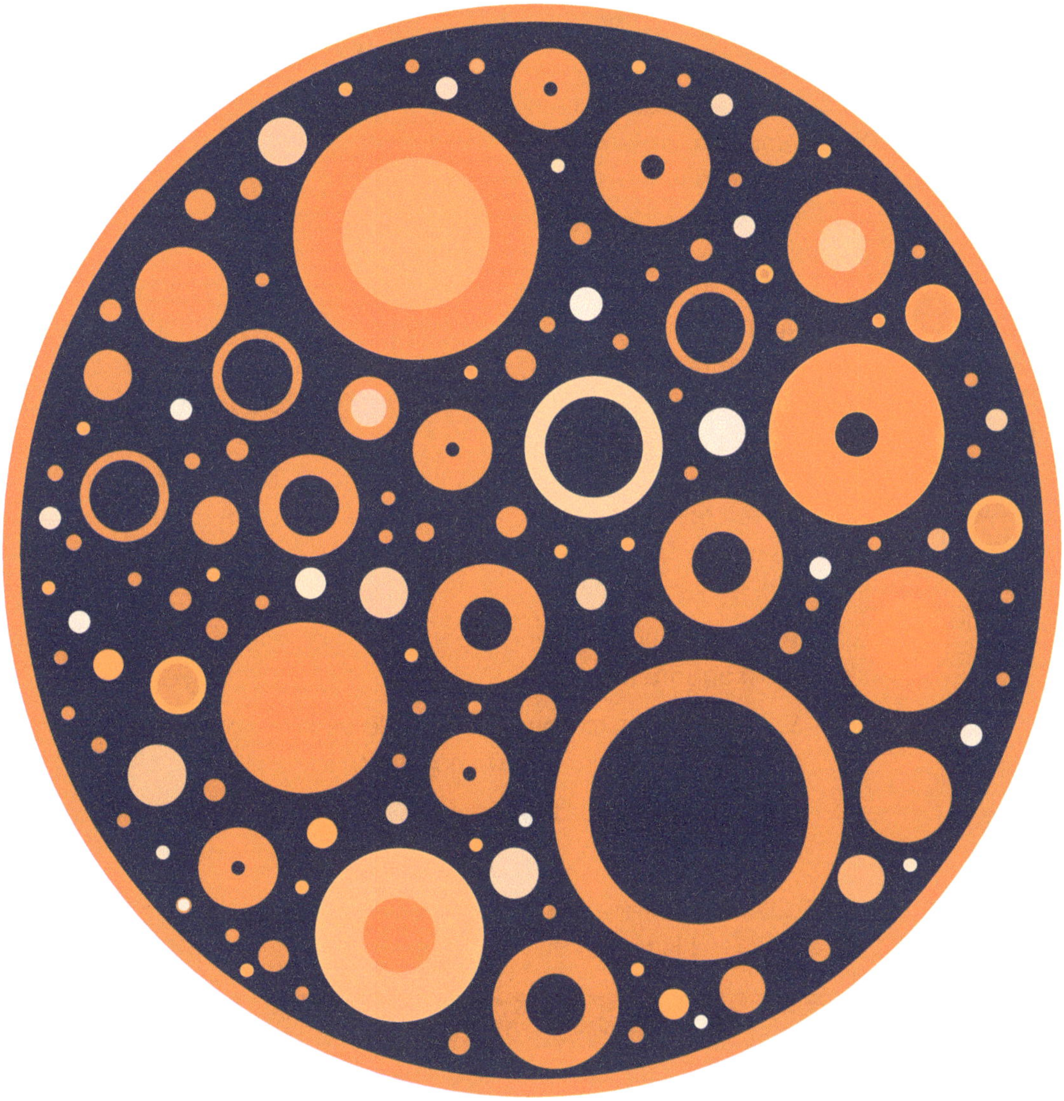

Lesson 2

God Is Most Important

"You must not have any other god but me" (Exodus 20:3).

Discover Exodus 20:3

If you were to rank the most important things in your life, what's number one? Your family? Your home? Your favorite song? Chocolate chip cookies?

Since God is the source of those good things, God is truly most important. God is God, and nothing can be ranked better or more powerful or more essential than a relationship with him.

Exodus 20:3 kicks off a list of important rules for God's people—in ancient times and today. In one sentence, God establishes who is most important in this world and in our lives. It's not a sun god or a god of the sea or any other thing God made or gave to his creation. It's THE one true God—the Creator and Giver of all good things.

God is most important. We can be grateful for the things God made, but God himself takes the cake. As his children, we center our lives on him. Understanding God's importance in our lives is at the heart of this lesson. As you lead, remember this.

- When it comes to being a good teacher, your own friendship with God is most important.
- When it comes to connecting Bible truth to young hearts, relying on the Holy Spirit's work is most important.
- More than the words you say, the way you model God's love and grace is most important.

God is most important. So trust God. Honor God. Help kids see how important God is to you and how important they are to God.

PRAYER

Oh God, you hold all things together—including this lesson. May my friendship with you be my most important priority today.

Fun Fact

Did you know that the word *exodus* means "to go out" or "to depart"? The Bible book of Exodus tells how God's people, the Israelites, departed Egypt and went out toward their new home in the Promised Land. And the book of Exodus tells about all sorts of adventures along the way. You'll mention several of those adventures in today's Bible Discovery.

Lesson Overview

Bible Verse: Exodus 20:3 | **Bible Point:** God is most important. *(It's true!)* | **Bible Exploration:** Exodus 13:21; 16; 17:1-6; 20

Lesson-at-a-Glance

Play Together (10-15 minutes)
Build something with blocks and/or play Simon Says.

Talk Together | Pray Together (10 minutes)
Talk about how you're feeling today, then pray and talk with God about it.

Bible Discovery (10-15 minutes)
Find and read Exodus 23:3 together, use blocks to explore important things God gave the Israelites, and talk about what makes God most important in our lives.

Wonder What Stations (15-20 minutes)
Choose and move through the following activities:
- Let's Play: Play card games or board games together, noting the important rules.
- Try This: Use wooden blocks to explore how God holds all things together.
- Create: Make a paper chain craft to show important people in your life.

Review Together (5 minutes)
Explore a Jesus Connection, work together to create actions for words in the Bible verse, and give out Here & Home papers.

Supply List

- ☐ Bible bookmarked at Exodus 20:3
- ☐ All Together Tasks labels (1 sheet for every 8 kids) (on page 8)
- ☐ Feelings Charts (1 for every 2 kids) (on page 9)
- ☐ Here & Home papers (1 per child) (on page 31)

Wonder What Bin Contents
- ☐ wooden blocks (at least 3 different sizes)
- ☐ familiar card games or board games
- ☐ construction paper strips
- ☐ clear tape or staplers
- ☐ crayons
- ☐ eye stickers

The "Wonder What Bin"

This supply box is a key part of each All Together Sunday School lesson. It will store all the toys and supplies needed for the Play Together activities and Wonder What Stations. Each week, kids will "wonder what" is in store for them! Your Wonder What Bin could be a storage bin, a toy box, or any large container.

Lesson 2   23

All Together Tasks

Supplies: All Together Tasks labels (1 sheet for every 8 kids)

As kids arrive, explain the special jobs and encourage each child to choose one to do today. Download and print the All Together Tasks labels or copy them from page 8, and let kids choose the jobs they want to do. It's okay if more than one child has the same job or if one child has a few jobs. Teachers can have another job, too!

Kids choose from the following jobs:

Ready Reader is ready and willing to read a Bible verse aloud.

Prayer Person prays aloud nice and loud so everyone can hear.

Happy Helpers jump at the chance to hand out supplies and clean up stuff.

Befrienders are on the lookout for those who need help and support.

Greeters say, "Hello and welcome!" to everyone as they arrive and "Have a good day!" to everyone as they leave.

Play Together (10-15 minutes)

Play with the kids, using their favorite toys and games to help introduce the Bible Point. Choose one or both activities.

Supplies:
- Wonder What Bin

Who's in Charge?

Work together to build something with blocks. It could be a maze to walk through, an obstacle to hop over, or a tower to knock down! Designate an "architect" who is in charge of coming up with what to build and do. After one plan is complete, choose another architect who'll be in charge of the next construction project!

Ask: Architects, how did you feel as you led your friends?

Ask: Builders, what was it like to follow someone else's instructions?

Say: Architects may have felt important because people listened to them and gladly did what they said to do. Today we'll explore a Bible verse that tells us who is most important. It's good—and even fun—to do things God's way because <u>God is most important</u>.

Simon Says

Play Simon Says, but before you do, review the rules so everyone knows what's important to remember about the game. Play several rounds, inviting different kids to be "Simon."

Ask: What's important to remember when playing Simon Says?

Say: Games are more fun when we know how to play. God gave people rules to follow, too, and we'll hear about one of them today. The rule helps people remember that <u>God is most important</u>.

24 All Together Sunday School Book 1

Talk Together (5 minutes)

> Kids talk in pairs about how they're feeling today.

Say: Today we'll talk with God and hear what God has to say to us through words in the Bible. But first, let's talk to each other. God made people in a special way. One thing that's special about us is having emotions. Emotions are how your body and your heart feel. In fact, we often call emotions "feelings." Let's talk about how we are feeling today with a friend.

Form pairs, and give each pair a Feelings Chart and a crayon. Have partners each circle the face that reflects how they're feeling in this moment and then tell their partners why they chose that face. Be sure to pair up with a child, too, so you can tell how *you're* feeling today!

Supplies:
- Feelings Charts (1 for every 2 kids)
- crayons

Download and print or make one copy of the Feelings Chart on page 9 for every two people. Instead of printing each week, consider placing the charts in plastic sheet protectors. Then kids can use dry-erase markers to mark how they're feeling. Simply clean off the markings for next week!

Pray Together (5 minutes)

> Kids tell God how they're feeling and pray a prayer all together.

Say: Feelings come and go based on what's happening around us. But God's love for us never changes. We can pray and tell God about anything—even our feelings!

Philippians 4:6 says, "Pray about everything. Tell God what you need, and thank him for all he has done."

Like we just talked with our friends, we can talk with God. We'll silently pray and tell God how we're feeling today. After our thinking prayer, we'll pray a special prayer all together.

Invite kids to get comfortable and close their eyes as they pray.

Pray: Dear God, we want to tell you how we feel today and why we feel that way. Pause for several moments of silent prayer. **Thanks for listening, God.**

Say: Now let's pray all together. We'll ask God to guide our time together today.

Watch and do what I do! After each sentence, I'll pause and we'll say the words "All together" together!

Pray: Dear God,

> **May we love** [make the shape of a heart with your hands] **you and each other.** ("All together!")
>
> **May we listen** [cup hand behind ear] **to you and each other.** ("All together!")
>
> **May we learn** [point to brain] **about you and each other.** ("All together!")
>
> **May we laugh and have fun** [high-five a friend] **with you and each other.** ("All together!")
>
> **Thanks for bringing us** ("All together!") **today. Amen.**

This prayer will set the tone for your time together each lesson. Each sentence helps to communicate the values in your classroom and invites God to help everyone do their part, no matter their age! When behavior challenges arise, you can guide kids back to this prayer, to steer them toward loving behaviors.

📖 Bible Discovery (15 minutes)

Find and read a verse together, explore its Bible context, and talk about stories in the Bible that reinforce the main idea of the verse.

Supplies:
- Bible bookmarked at Exodus 20:3
- wooden blocks (at least 3 different sizes)

Find and read Exodus 20:3.

Say: Let's hear a Bible verse that'll help us get to know God even better. Today we'll explore Exodus 20:3.

The Bible is made up of Bible *books*, *chapters*, and *verses*. Exodus is the book, the number "20" is the chapter, and the number "3" is the verse.

This verse comes from a passage in the Bible called the "Ten Commandments." The Ten Commandments are the rules God gave his people, called the Israelites, a long time ago. Let's read one now.

Invite the Ready Reader to read the verse from your marked Bible. Have everyone clap to thank the Ready Reader for reading.

Back when God said these words, people thought there were lots of gods. A sun god, a moon god, a god that made crops grow, even a god of the sea! God made all those things—they didn't come from fake gods. So God wanted the Israelites to know the truth: God is in charge of everything, and God is most important! *(It's true!)*

That's our Bible Point today. So every time you hear the words "God is most important," give two thumbs up and say, "It's true!" To practice, repeat the Bible Point and response several times.

When something is important, it's very valuable. Important things are a big deal to us because we need them a lot.

Ask: What important things do you need? Share an answer from your life, then invite others to share.

Line up wooden blocks as you explore how God took care of the Israelites.

Say: The Israelites had a lot of important things in their lives, too. And the one true God gave them all those things. Let's find out more about those important things. We'll imagine these blocks are important things God gave the Israelites.

Hold up a larger block first. **Imagine these blocks are the important *things* God gave. Right before God gave them special rules, God gave his people food called "manna" (Exodus 16). Manna was kind of like crackers. God also gave them meat to eat.**

Ask: What foods do you like to eat? Share an answer from your life, then invite others to share.

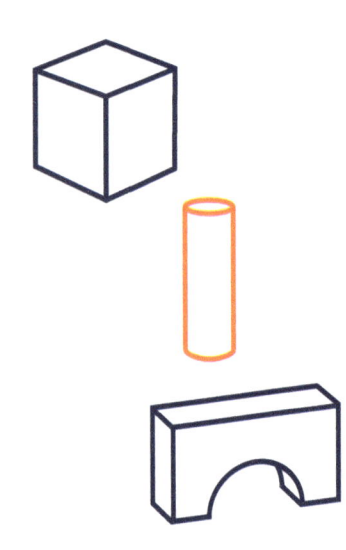

26 All Together Sunday School Book 1

Say: **God gave the Israelites water when they were thirsty, too** (Exodus 17:1-6). **Sometimes the Israelites grumbled and complained about their food. And I suppose we do, too, sometimes. Still God takes care of us.** Have kids line up all the largest blocks to show the things God gave.

Hold up blocks that are a little smaller to represent the important things God did. **God *did* important things for the Israelites, too. And as they traveled from a place called Egypt to a new home, God showed them where to go—that's important! God gave them a cloud to follow during the day and a fiery light to follow at night** (Exodus 13:21). Have kids line up those blocks near the larger blocks to show the important things God did for the Israelites.

Show the smallest blocks. **And God gave the Israelites important people, too! They had leaders named Moses and Miriam and Aaron. They had family members like brothers and sisters and moms and dads and grandmas and grandpas.** Have kids line up those blocks to represent the important people God gave the Israelites.

Ask: Who is an important person God put in your life?

Say: I'm glad God has given us such wonderful people to love and care for us. Look at all those blocks. God gave the Israelites all sorts of important things. And <u>God is most important</u>. *(It's true!)*

But God *did not* give his people other gods to love and worship. Other gods aren't real. In Exodus 20:3 God tells his people what isn't important. God said, "You must not have any other god but me."

God said fake gods are not important. God is! God is the biggest and most important of all. God is the giver of all things because <u>God is most important</u>. *(It's true!)* **Let's make these blocks spell out who is most important.** Work together to spell out "God" with blocks.

Talk about important things God gives people today.

Back when God gave the Israelites and their leader, named Moses, the Ten Commandments, all the different fake gods seemed important to people who lived back then. The fake gods were special because people thought they helped them with everyday life.

Today we may not think fake gods are important in our lives, but we do think other things are important.

Ask: I wonder, what are important things in our lives today? Share a kid-friendly example from your own life, like laptops, cars, or dishwashers! Then invite responses from the whole group.

Say: God is the one who gives us those good things. We can love and enjoy those things *and* remember who gave them to us—the one true God!

Pray together.

We center our lives on things that are special to us. That means no matter where we are, what we have, or what we do, God is in the middle of it. Let's circle up around the blocks that spell "God" and ask God to help us center our lives on him.

Prayer Person, will you talk with God for us to end the prayer? I'll give you a signal when it's time.

Pray: Dear God, you are most important. Without you, we'd be super sad and super lost. You give us what we need—and then some! Thanks for filling our lives with big, important things. You are big and special, and we love you a lot.

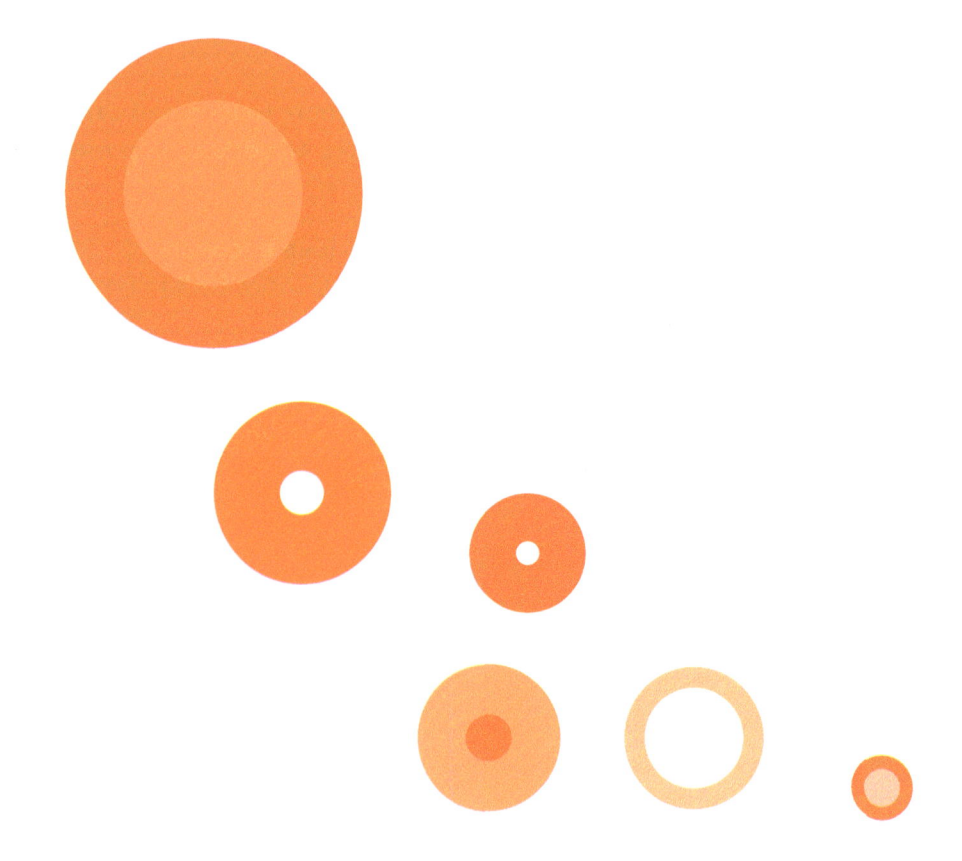

Wonder What Stations (15-20 minutes)

Kids will wonder and wander their way through these three free-flowing application activities. Young kids may gravitate toward some things while older kids are drawn to others.

Supplies:
- Wonder What Bin

Say: Let's keep exploring Exodus 20:3 with the items in this Wonder What Bin. You'll have three choices—I wonder what you'll choose to do first!

Dramatically re-reveal what's inside the Wonder What Bin, and explain these three different options for kids to choose during a free-play time. After 15-20 minutes, tell kids you'll be cleaning up the Wonder What Stations in about a minute. Have Happy Helpers return supplies to the Wonder What Bin.

Let's Play

Play familiar card games or board games together.

Ask: Are you glad there are rules for this game? Tell why.

Ask: Do you think the Israelites were glad to have God's rules? Tell why.

Say: God's rules were good for his people. God's rules are important because they come from God. And <u>God is most important</u>. *(It's true!)*

Try This

Stack wooden blocks to make a square tower, then take turns trying to carefully remove blocks one by one.

Say: In this game, we have to think about which block is most important. If we pull out an important block that's holding a lot of weight, it all falls apart. Another verse in the Bible says this about God: "He existed before anything else, and he holds all creation together" (Colossians 1:17). That means <u>God is most important</u>! *(It's true!)* **God holds everything together.**

Ask: Tell about a time things felt like they were falling apart. How did God help "hold you together" during that time?

As kids play, meander around the area, using these questions and comments to connect each activity to today's Bible verse and Bible Point.

Create

Make a chain of paper people. On construction paper strips, attach eye stickers, then draw a face to represent an important person in your life. Then loop the strips together and staple them together.

Ask: Who's on your chain? Why are those people important to you?

Say: God gave 10 important rules to follow. Those rules help us love God and love other people. <u>God is most important</u>. *(It's true!)* **And God gives us important people to love and care for us. Following God's rules helps us love God and people really well.**

Lesson 2

Review Together (5 minutes)

> Explore a Jesus Connection and work together to create actions for words in the Bible verse.

Supplies:
- Here & Home papers (1 per child)
- crayons

Say: God gave his people, called the Israelites, special rules to follow, called the Ten Commandments. God's Son, Jesus, made a way for us to be God's people today, so the Ten Commandments are special rules we follow, too!

The first commandment is Exodus 20:3: "You must not have any other god but me." God wanted his people back then and people today to know that God is most important. *(It's true!)* God is the one true God who gives us all good things.

Let's create some actions to do as we say Exodus 20:3 all together. Rather than *me* telling you what to do, you kids can create the actions for us. You're in charge!

Invite kids to work together to make up actions for these words:

- You
- must not have
- but me

Say Exodus 20:3 together with actions: **"You must not have any other god but me."**

God is most important because God is the one true God. *(It's true!)* And it's so cool to think that God, the most important of all, loves and cares for people—including you and me. We are important to God!

Take some time to affirm kids by name, saying: [Child's name], **you are important to God.**

Here & Home

Give kids each the Here & Home paper on page 31. Invite them to color and complete the Bible verse page now, and point out the activity for them to lead their parents in at home.

God Is Most Important

Here

Color this picture as you think about the Bible verse. Choose three colors to use. Decide which one will be most important, and use that one the most.

"You must not have any other God but me."
Exodus 20:3

Here & Home Lesson 2

Home

God Is Most Important

"You must not have any other god but me" (Exodus 20:3).

If you were to rank the most important things in your life, what's number one? Your family? Your home? Your favorite song? Chocolate chip cookies?

Since God is the source of those good things, God is truly most important. God is God, and nothing can be ranked better or more powerful or more special than a relationship with him.

Exodus 20:3 kicks off a list of important rules for God's people. In one sentence, God shows who is most important in this world and in our lives. It's not a fake sun god or a fake god of the sea or any other thing God made or gave to his creation. It's THE one true God—the Creator and Giver of all good things.

God is most important. We can be grateful for the things God made, but God himself takes the cake. As his children, we center our lives on him.

Fun Fact

Did you know that the word *exodus* means "to go out" or "to depart"? Exodus tells how God's people, the Israelites, departed Egypt and went out toward their new home in the Promised Land. And the book of Exodus tells about all sorts of adventures along the way.

Think & Talk

What's something important that happened today?

Read & Do

Read Colossians 1:17. Then make something that holds together. It could be a Lego tower, a peanut butter and jelly sandwich, or shoelaces! How have you noticed God holding your family together this week?

Say & Pray

As a family, hold hands. Pray and thank God for the important things and people in your lives.

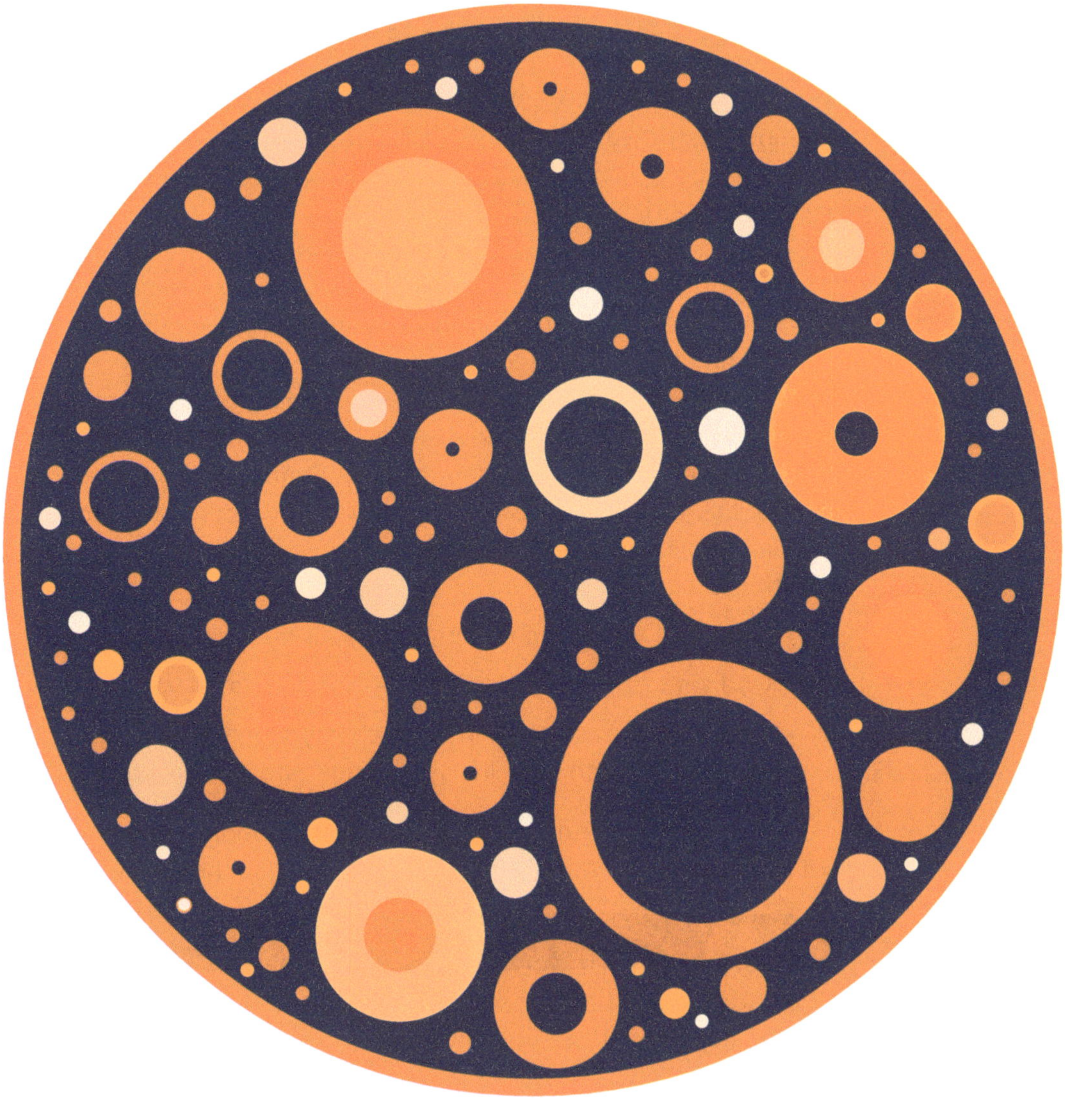

Lesson 3

God Sees Our Hearts

"People judge by the outward appearance, but the Lord looks at the heart" (1 Samuel 16:7).

Discover 1 Samuel 16:7

God sees our hearts. For some, that truth brings great relief and comfort. On the flip side, though, this awareness can also stir up feelings of shame or guilt. Upon hearing this verse, kids of all ages may worry, "Is my heart good enough for God?"

Today, let's lean toward the comfort that comes from being fully known by the Maker of the universe and completely loved no matter what tough stuff our hearts are working through. God sees our hearts—the good, the bad, and the ugly. And he loves us. Period.

When we devote our hearts to God, God is ready to work through us in amazing ways! David was the chosen king, not because of his "dark handsomeness" or his "beautiful eyes" (1 Samuel 16:12). David was the right man for the job because God saw David's devotion to God and his ways.

Similarly, if your heart trusts God, then you're the right person to lead this lesson.

- God sees your preparation—and your frazzled moments.
- God sees your love for his kids—and the times you lose your patience.
- God sees the potential in each child you lead and just might already be working through kids' lives in unique and special ways.

God sees our hearts. So let's trust that, through your time together, God will fill kids' hearts with his love and his grace as they grow to trust him more.

PRAYER

Oh God, search me and know my heart. Thanks for your grace that helps my heart trust you more and more. Amen.

Fun Fact

You aren't the first to tell this Bible story. The Apostle Paul told it to Christians in Antioch, too! Check out Acts 13:22. Paul said that God called David "a man after my own heart."

Lesson Overview

📖 **Bible Verse:** 1 Samuel 16:7 | **Bible Point:** God sees our hearts. *(It's true!)* | **Bible Exploration:** 1 Samuel 16:1-13

Lesson-at-a-Glance

Play Together (10-15 minutes)
Choose a favorite car to race and/or play a game based on what colors kids are wearing.

Talk Together | Pray Together (10 minutes)
Talk about how you're feeling today, then pray and talk with God about it.

Bible Discovery (10-15 minutes)
Find and read 1 Samuel 16:7 together, have a messenger help explain a prophet's job, and use cups to find out how God picked David to be king.

Wonder What Stations (15-20 minutes)
Choose and move through the following activities:
- Create: Make a heart craft to help talk with God about what's on your heart.
- Imagine That: Choose a toy car that best represents something about you—then race it!
- Let's Play: Play the Telephone game to communicate a message.

Review Together (5 minutes)
Explore a Jesus Connection, work together to create actions for words in the Bible verse, and give out Here & Home papers.

Supply List

- ☐ Bible bookmarked at 1 Samuel 16:7
- ☐ All Together Tasks labels (1 sheet for every 8 kids) (on page 8)
- ☐ Feelings Charts (1 for every 2 kids) (on page 9)
- ☐ 8 colorful disposable cups
- ☐ 8 small foam or paper hearts
- ☐ permanent marker
- ☐ Here & Home papers (1 per child) (on page 43)
- ☐ crayons

Wonder What Bin Contents
- ☐ small toy cars (like Hot Wheels or Monster Jam trucks)
- ☐ racetracks (optional)
- ☐ washable markers
- ☐ large foam or paper hearts

The "Wonder What Bin"

This supply box is a key part of each All Together Sunday School lesson. It will store all the toys and supplies needed for the Play Together activities and Wonder What Stations. Each week, kids will "wonder what" is in store for them! Your Wonder What Bin could be a storage bin, a toy box, or any large container.

Lesson 3 35

All Together Tasks

Supplies: All Together Tasks labels (1 sheet for every 8 kids)

As kids arrive, explain the special jobs and encourage each child to choose one to do today. Download and print the All Together Tasks labels or copy them from page 8, and let kids choose the jobs they want to do. It's okay if more than one child has the same job or if one child has a few jobs. Teachers can have another job, too!

Kids choose from the following jobs:

Ready Reader is ready and willing to read a Bible verse aloud.

Prayer Person prays aloud nice and loud so everyone can hear.

Happy Helpers jump at the chance to hand out supplies and clean up stuff.

Befrienders are on the lookout for those who need help and support.

Greeters say, "Hello and welcome!" to everyone as they arrive and "Have a good day!" to everyone as they leave.

Play Together (10-15 minutes)

Play with the kids, using their favorite toys and games to help introduce the Bible Point. Choose one or both activities.

Choose Your Racecar

Supplies:
- Wonder What Bin

Work together to design a racetrack using tracks, the floor, or a sloped surface. Take turns choosing a car to race. Have several races, giving different people a chance to choose cars and win.

Ask: Which car is your favorite? Why did you choose that car when it was your turn to race?

Ask: In a real car race, which is more important: the inside or the outside of the car? Tell why.

Say: In real cars, though, the strength of the engine inside is more important than the outside decorations. Today we'll explore a Bible verse that says what's inside a person is more important than what we see on the outside. We'll discover that <u>God sees our hearts</u>.

Color Shift

Remind older kids to watch out for younger friends as they hurry to a new seat.

Place chairs in a circle with one less chair than people playing. The person without a chair will stand in the center of the circle and call out a color. Anyone wearing clothing of that color must move to a different chair while the person in the middle attempts to sit in an empty chair. Whoever is left without a chair goes to the center of the circle and calls out a new color. Callers may call one, two, or even three colors at a time, or they may shout, "Any color!" and everyone must move to a new chair.

36   All Together Sunday School Book 1

Say: Our game was based on what we're wearing on the outside. I wonder… how could we change the game and focus instead on what we're like on the inside? Invite ideas from older kids. For example, you could call out favorite TV shows, what people ate for breakfast, or how they are feeling today. Then play a round that way.

Ask: How were the two rounds of this game different? Did you like one version better than the other? Tell why.

Say: When we played with colors, we could see if someone should move or not. But we can't see people's feelings and favorites. Today we'll find out that God sees our hearts. God knows our feelings and our favorites—and he loves us so much.

Talk Together (5 minutes)

Kids talk in pairs about how they're feeling today.

Say: Today we'll talk with God and hear what God has to say to us through words God gave to the writers of the Bible. But first, let's talk together.

People can see what you're wearing today, but they may not be able to see how you're feeling. It's good to talk about the feelings in our hearts with a friend. So let's do that now. How are you feeling today?

Form pairs, and give each pair a Feelings Chart and a crayon. Have partners each circle the face that reflects how they're feeling in this moment and then tell their partners why they chose that face. Be sure to find a partner, too, and participate with the kids as they chat.

Pray Together (5 minutes)

Kids tell God how they're feeling and pray a prayer all together.

Say: Thanks for talking with a friend! In the Bible, we read that we can pray and tell God anything. You'll see the words of that Bible verse printed on the Feelings Chart. If you'd like to read along, please do! Or you can simply listen as I read God's words.

Philippians 4:6 says, "Pray about everything. Tell God what you need, and thank him for all he has done."

Like we just talked with our friends, we can talk with God! Let's practice doing that now! We'll silently pray and tell God how we're feeling today. We won't pray with our voices—instead we'll just think a prayer to God for a little bit. After our thinking prayer, we'll pray a special prayer out loud, all together.

Invite kids to get comfortable and close their eyes as they pray.

Pray: Dear God, we want to tell you how our hearts feel today and why we feel that way. Pause for several moments of silent prayer. Thanks for listening, God.

Supplies:
- Feelings Charts (1 for every 2 kids)
- crayons

Download and print or make one copy of the Feelings Chart on page 9 for every two people. Instead of printing each week, consider placing the charts in plastic sheet protectors. Then kids can use dry-erase markers to mark how they're feeling. Simply clean off the markings for next week!

This prayer will set the tone for your time together each lesson. Each sentence helps to communicate the values in your classroom and invites God to help everyone do their part, no matter their age! When behavior challenges arise, you can guide kids back to this prayer, to steer them toward loving behaviors.

Say: Now let's pray all together. We'll ask God to guide our time together today.

Watch and do what I do! After each sentence, I'll pause and we'll say the words "All together" together!

Pray: Dear God,

May we love [make the shape of a heart with your hands] you and each other. ("All together!")

May we listen [cup hand behind ear] to you and each other. ("All together!")

May we learn [point to brain] about you and each other. ("All together!")

May we laugh and have fun [high-five a friend] with you and each other. ("All together!")

Thanks for bringing us ("All together!") today. Amen.

📖 Bible Discovery (15 minutes)

Find and read a verse together, explore its Bible context, and talk about stories in the Bible that reinforce the main idea of the verse.

Supplies:
- Bible bookmarked at 1 Samuel 16:7
- 8 colorful disposable cups
- 8 small foam or paper hearts
- permanent marker

Find and read 1 Samuel 16:7.

Say: Let's hear a Bible verse that'll help us get to know God even better. Today we'll explore 1 Samuel 16:7.

The Bible is one book, but it's made up of separate *books*, *chapters*, and *verses*. There are two "Samuel" books in the Bible—1 Samuel and 2 Samuel. These books are filled with stories about kings who were in charge of God's people. Some were good kings, and some were not-so-good kings. Let's hear 1 Samuel 16:7.

Invite the Ready Reader to read the verse from your marked Bible. Have everyone high-five the Ready Reader as a way to say, "Thanks for reading!"

Ask: What does this verse tell us about God?

Say: This verse tells us that <u>God sees our hearts</u>. That's our Bible Point today. So every time you hear the words "God sees our hearts," give two thumbs up and say, "It's true!" To practice, repeat the Bible Point and response several times.

Listen to this part of the verse again: "People judge by outward appearance, but the Lord looks at the heart."

"The Lord" is a name for God. God first said these words in today's Bible verse to a man named Samuel. Samuel had been friends with God since he was just a young boy. God spoke to Samuel, and Samuel told people messages from God.

God would speak. Samuel would listen. Then Samuel would tell others, and they'd do what God said—most of the time.

38   All Together Sunday School Book 1

Speak through a messenger.

I wonder, who'll be my "messenger" like Samuel and help me tell this Bible story? Choose a willing person to be your messenger. Whisper the bolded text to the messenger, and have that person loudly repeat what you say.

Samuel did what God told him to do.
(Samuel did what God told him to do.)

God told Samuel that his people could have a king.
(God told Samuel that his people could have a king.)

Saul was the first king of Israel.
(Saul was the first king of Israel.)

But King Saul didn't work out so well.
(But King Saul didn't work out so well.)

You know,
(You know,)

This could take a while.
(This could take a while.)

I think I'll just tell the rest of the story myself.
(I think I'll just tell the rest of the story myself.)

Thanks, messenger!
(Thanks, messenger!)

Have everyone clap for the volunteer.

Ask: Messenger, what was it like to listen and tell people messages?

Ask: Everyone else, what was it like to hear information from a messenger?

Say: In the Bible, people who gave messages from God were called prophets. Samuel was a prophet. A prophet's job wasn't easy. And sometimes people were confused by what prophets told them God said.

Use cups and foam hearts to find God's new king.

King Saul may have *seemed* like a good choice for king, but his heart didn't trust God very well. So God would tell Samuel who the new king should be. Ready Reader, will you please read another verse in 1 Samuel for us?

Ready Reader reads 1 Samuel 16:1 aloud.

So off Samuel went to Jesse's house. Let's sit in a circle and imagine our bodies are the walls of Jesse's house. Sit together in a circle. **Jesse had a bunch of kids. Let's invite them to the story.** Ask Happy Helpers to count out eight cups and place them in the center of your group's "house."

These cups represent Jesse's sons. Since we're pretending they're people, let's give them each a heart. The heart is an organ in the body that pumps blood. But we also talk about our hearts as a way to show who we are inside, what we're feeling, and what we love. Have kids help you place a foam heart inside each cup.

Lesson 3   39

Hold up one of the cups. **This guy is the youngest son. His name is David. He wasn't around when Samuel showed up to pick a king. He was out with the sheep.** Have kids "baa" like sheep and pass around the David cup, then place the cup outside the circle.

You sheep sound *baaaaad*! Let's bring our attention back to Samuel and the brothers in the house. When Samuel saw the oldest brother, he thought, "Surely this is the man God wants to be king!" But that wasn't God's message! Instead, God said the words in our Bible verse.

Read aloud 1 Samuel 16:7.

All these cups have hearts. And all Jesse's sons had hearts too. Perhaps their hearts weren't *bad*. But God was looking for a special something inside.

Ask: **What do you think God wanted to see inside the next king's heart?** Invite responses from the whole group.

Say: <u>**God sees our hearts**</u>. *(It's true!)* **God could see who trusted him and who would obey him. God's next leader needed to have a heart that cared about the things God cared about. Let's check all the other brothers' hearts. Is there anything about God on them?** Have kids look inside all the cups, confirming the blank hearts.

Oh! That's right! The stinky sheep brother! Have kids pass you the David cup again. **Friendship with God had changed David's heart. I'll write G-O-D on this cup's heart.** Use a permanent marker to write "God" on the heart. **See David's heart? God is with David!** Invite kids to look and see "David's" heart.

All the brothers had hearts. But God picked David because he saw something special in David's heart. God saw that David would be a good, godly leader for his people. Let's cheer for king David! Lead kids in shouting "Hip, hip, hooray!"

Pray together.

You know, we all have hearts, too. <u>**God sees our hearts**</u>. *(It's true!)* **God knows what's going on in our hearts. And through Jesus, God has made a way for our hearts to be filled with his love—forever!**

Ask: **Who can show us how to make the shape of a heart with our hands? Any ideas?** Invite kids to show you and each other different ways to form a heart shape.

Say: **Very cool! Let's make heart hands and have an eyes-open prayer and talk with God about our hearts.** Ask the Prayer Person to pray a simple prayer or simply say "Amen!"

Pray: **Dear God, when you look at our hearts, may you see our love for you, our trust in you, and our gratefulness to be called your kids. Thank you.**

Wonder What Stations (15-20 minutes)

> Kids will wonder and wander their way through these three free-flowing application activities. Young kids may gravitate toward some things while older kids are drawn to others.

Say: Let's keep exploring 1 Samuel 16:7 with the items in this Wonder What Bin. You'll have three choices—I wonder what you'll choose to do first!

Dramatically re-reveal what's inside the Wonder What Bin, and explain these three different options for kids to choose during a free-play time. After 15-20 minutes, tell kids you'll be cleaning up the Wonder What Stations in about a minute. Have Happy Helpers return supplies to the Wonder What Bin.

Supplies:
- Wonder What Bin

Create

On one side of your foam heart, draw or write words that describe people you love and things you love to do! Then, on the other side of the heart, write or draw things you don't love so much or people you need God to help you love.

Ask: How does your heart feel when you are with these people and do these things?

Say: God sees our hearts. *(It's true!)* Gods knows all about the things you love *and* the things you don't love so much. We can talk with God about anything that's on our hearts. God sees our hearts and loves us no matter what.

As kids play, meander around the area, using these questions and comments to connect each activity to today's Bible verse and Bible Point.

Imagine That

Race cars again! But this time, choose a car that represents you—that reminds you of something you like or shows what your heart loves. Maybe you'd pick a red car because it reminds you of your favorite fruit. Before each race, explain why you chose that car.

Ask: What car best represents you? How is it like you?

Say: Thanks for showing us a little bit of your hearts—through race cars! God sees our hearts. *(It's true!)* So God knows all the things you shared—and more.

Let's Play

Play the Telephone game! Stand in a line. The first person will think of a silly sentence, then whisper it to the next person in line. Whisper the silliness down the line, then have the last person say it aloud. Encourage Happy Helpers and Befrienders to be ready to give message ideas to friends when needed.

Ask: How did the silly messages change?

Say: Like you passed along messages from friends, prophets passed along messages from God. God knew how people would hear and understand messages because God sees our hearts. *(It's true!)*

Lesson 3   41

Review Together (5 minutes)

> Explore a Jesus Connection and work together to create actions for words in the Bible verse.

Supplies:
- Here & Home papers (1 per child)
- crayons
- washable markers

Say: God created each person in a special way—including you and me. God gave us hearts that care about things. Our hearts are drawn to certain things and certain people and to Jesus, God's special Son who make a way for us to be close friends with God forever.

You may not be the next king of [your town's name], **but when God looks at your heart, he might see that you're the perfect fit for other jobs. When God sees that you love and trust in him, God works through your heart and life in really cool ways!** Mention a few specific ways God has shown you his love through the kids you lead.

Let's create some actions to do as we say 1 Samuel 16:7 all together. Rather than *me* telling you what to do, you kids can create the actions for us. You're in charge!

Invite kids to work together to make up actions for these words:

- people
- outward appearance
- the Lord
- looks
- heart

Say 1 Samuel 16:7 together with actions:
"People judge by outward appearance, but the Lord looks at the heart."

<u>**God sees our hearts.**</u> *(It's true!)* **There is nothing in your heart that you need to hide from God. God sees you, knows you, and loves you. And God will help you know and love him more and more!**

Here & Home

Give kids each the Here & Home paper on page 43. Invite them to color and complete the Bible verse page now, and point out the activity for them to lead their parents in at home.

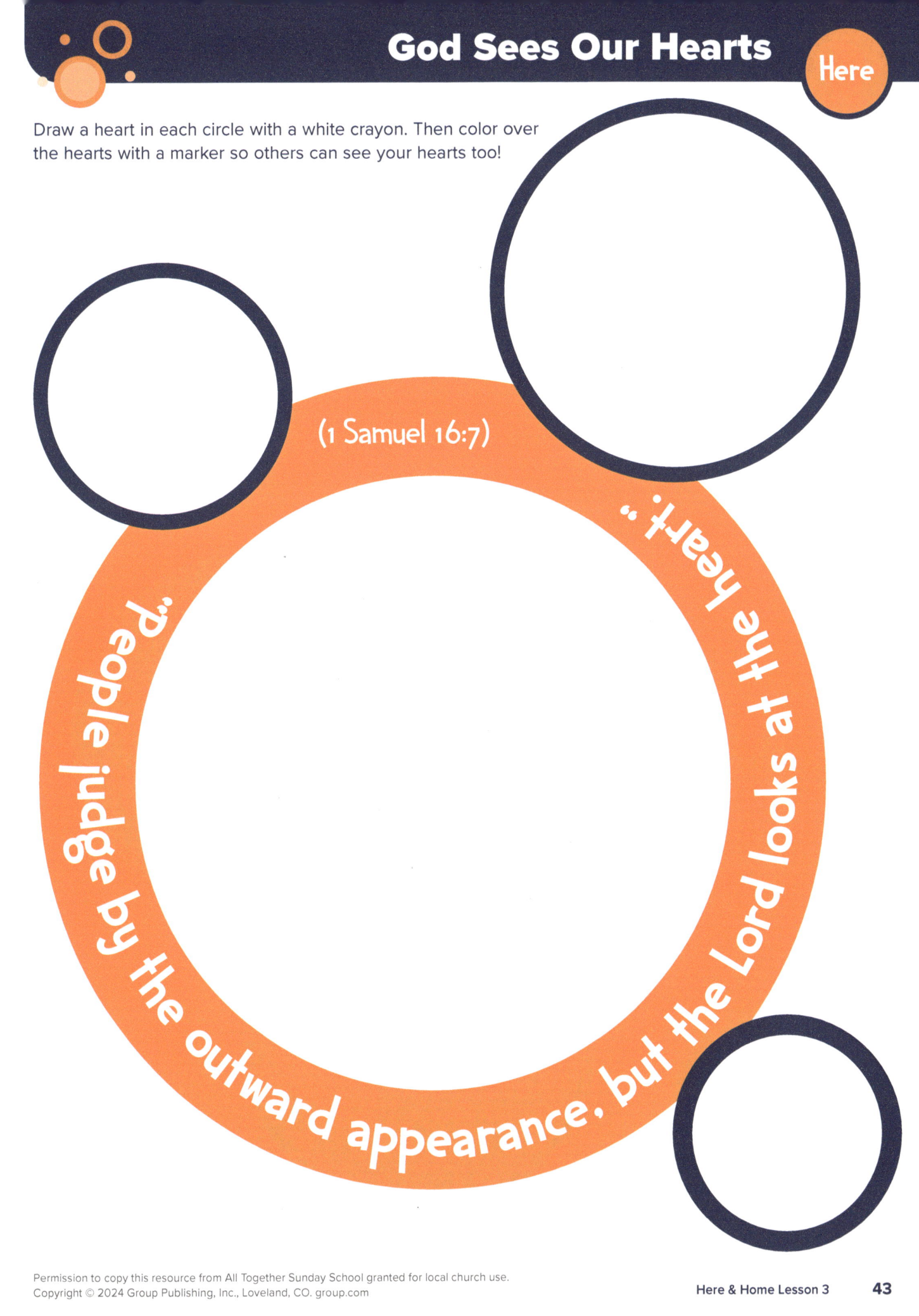

God Sees Our Hearts

Here

Draw a heart in each circle with a white crayon. Then color over the hearts with a marker so others can see your hearts too!

"People judge by the outward appearance, but the Lord looks at the heart." (1 Samuel 16:7)

Here & Home Lesson 3

Home

God Sees Our Hearts

"People judge by the outward appearance, but the Lord looks at the heart" (1 Samuel 16:7).

God sees our hearts. We are fully known by the Maker of the universe and completely loved no matter what tough stuff our hearts are working through. God sees our hearts—the good, the bad, and the ugly. And he loves us. Period.

When we devote our hearts to God, God is ready to work through us in amazing ways! David was the chosen king, not because of his "dark handsomeness" or his "beautiful eyes" (1 Samuel 16:12). When we read more about David, we find that his heart wasn't always pure and perfect. Still, David was the right man for the job because God saw David's devotion to God and his ways.

Fun Fact

The Apostle Paul told the story of Samuel anointing David as king. Check out Acts 13:22. Paul said that God called David "a man after my own heart."

Think & Talk

What was your favorite part of today?

Read & Do

Walk outside as you read Psalm 139:1-6. Use chalk to draw a heart on your sidewalk as a reminder that God sees you and goes before you this week.

Say & Pray

Ask God this question: What's something good you see in my family members' hearts? Listen for his answer. If you hear from God, share his message with your family.

Lesson 3   45

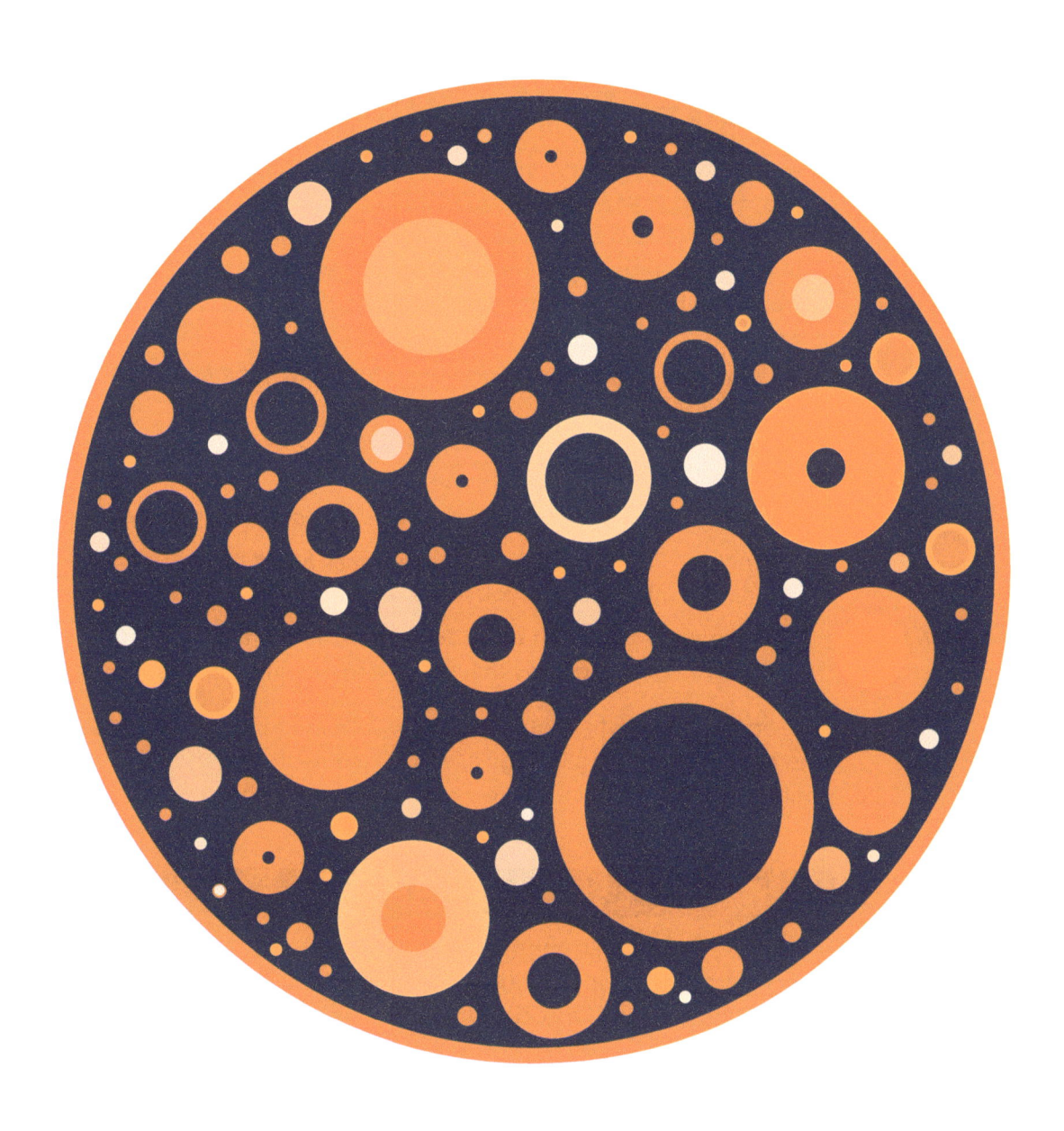

Lesson 4

God Takes Care of Us

"The Lord is my shepherd; I have all that I need" (Psalm 23:1).

Discover Psalm 23:1

It's a beautiful poem. Its words paint vivid pictures of the metaphorical mountains and valleys people encounter in life. It has inspired books. It's read at church services. It's recalled from memory in the dark of night. It's Psalm 23.

As you prepare for this lesson, stop reading the words on this page. Instead, read David's psalm aloud. Let yourself hear the words, for the first time or the 400th time.

(Really! Read Psalm 23 aloud from your favorite Bible translation now.)

God, our good shepherd, takes care of us. Under God's care, we have everything we need. And with God's guidance, *you* have everything you need to lead this lesson well.

- When you need to think quickly, God gives the insight you need.
- When you need to slow down and really listen to what's on kids' hearts, God gives the interest you need.
- When you need to let go of your agenda and have some fun with your young friends, God has the smiles and laughter you need.

God gives you what you need, little lamb. So trust God to guide you today. When you rest in God's loving care, you'll authentically show those you lead what it looks like to trust and rely on our good shepherd.

Fun Fact

According to the *Wycliff Bible Encyclopedia*, the shepherd's staff in Psalm 23 represents "security, protection, and perhaps the nearness of God." What object in your life reminds you of God's nearness in a similar way?

PRAYER

Lord, you are my shepherd who gives me everything I need. Pursue my heart with your goodness and unfailing love as your children and I follow you together today. In Jesus' name, amen.

Lesson Overview

Bible Verse: Psalm 23:1 | **Bible Point:** God takes care of us. *(It's true!)* | **Bible Exploration:** Psalm 23; 1 Samuel 17:32-37

Lesson-at-a-Glance

Play Together (10-15 minutes)
Play a game where you'll guide each other across the room and/or lead rhythms for everyone to repeat.

Talk Together | Pray Together (10 minutes)
Talk about how you're feeling today, then pray and talk with God about it.

Bible Discovery (10-15 minutes)
Find and read 1 Samuel 16:7 together, and shape chenille wires into pictures as you hear about David the shepherd and his adventures with sheep—and Goliath!

Wonder What Stations (15-20 minutes)
Choose and move through the following activities:
- **Create:** Make a maze, then carefully shepherd a water droplet through it.
- **Let's Play:** Play board games and consider how God guides people through ups and downs of life.
- **Try This:** Work together to guide a beach ball across the room and back without it hitting the ground.

Review Together (5 minutes)
Explore a Jesus Connection, work together to create actions for words in the Bible Verse, and give out Here & Home papers.

Supply List

- ☐ Bible bookmarked at Psalm 23:1
- ☐ All Together Tasks labels (1 sheet for every 8 kids) (on page 8)
- ☐ Feelings Charts (1 for every 2 kids) (on page 9)
- ☐ chenille wires
- ☐ child-safe scissors
- ☐ Here & Home papers (1 per child) (on page 55)

Wonder What Bin Contents
- ☐ beach ball
- ☐ simple board games like "Sorry!" or "Candy Land"
- ☐ copy paper
- ☐ crayons and markers
- ☐ large resealable plastic bags
- ☐ drinking straws
- ☐ small cups of water

The "Wonder What Bin"

This supply box is a key part of each All Together Sunday School lesson. It will store all the toys and supplies needed for the Play Together activities and Wonder What Stations. Each week, kids will "wonder what" is in store for them! Your Wonder What Bin could be a storage bin, a toy box, or any large container.

Lesson 4

All Together Tasks

Supplies: All Together Tasks labels (1 sheet for every 8 kids)

As kids arrive, explain the special jobs and encourage each child to choose one to do today. Download and print the All Together Tasks labels or copy them from page 8, and let kids choose the jobs they want to do. It's okay if more than one child has the same job or if one child has a few jobs. Teachers can have another job, too!

Kids choose from the following jobs:

Ready Reader is ready and willing to read a Bible verse aloud.

Prayer Person prays aloud nice and loud so everyone can hear.

Happy Helpers jump at the chance to hand out supplies and clean up stuff.

Befrienders are on the lookout for those who need help and support.

Greeters say, "Hello and welcome!" to everyone as they arrive and "Have a good day!" to everyone as they leave.

Play Together (10-15 minutes)

Play with the kids, using their favorite toys and games to help introduce the Bible Point. Choose one or both activities.

Supplies:
- Wonder What Bin

Lava!

Play a game like The Floor Is Lava. Use furniture in your room and items in the Wonder What Bin to make a path across the space. Help each other move along the path without touching the floor.

Ask: How did you take care of each other during this game?

Say: Today we'll explore a Bible verse that calls God our shepherd. A shepherd takes care of sheep. Sheep may not risk falling into lava, but they do need shepherds to help keep them out of danger. God is like our shepherd because God takes care of us.

Band Leader

Choose someone to be the "Band Leader." That person will invent a fun rhythm for everyone to repeat. The Band Leader can clap hands, pat a table, pat a friend's hand, or lead in other silly and creative ways. Take turns as the Band Leader, and cheer and encourage each other after each round.

Ask: What were your favorite ways to make a rhythm? What was it like to follow our leaders in this game?

Say: When someone leads us well, we have a blast and learn together. Today we'll discover that God leads our lives. When we choose to follow God, God takes care of us.

Talk Together (5 minutes)

> Kids talk in pairs about how they're feeling today.

Say: Today we'll talk with God and hear what God has to say to us through words in the Bible. But first, let's talk to each other and tell what's going on in our lives.

This Feelings Chart will give us a good way to start talking.

Form pairs, and give each pair a Feelings Chart and a crayon. Have partners each circle the face that reflects how they're feeling in this moment and then tell their partners why they chose that face. Be sure to find a partner, too, and participate with the kids as they chat.

Pray Together (5 minutes)

> Kids tell God how they're feeling and pray a prayer all together.

Say: We've had some good conversations! In the Bible, we read that we can pray and tell God anything, too. You'll see the words of that Bible verse printed on the Feelings Chart. If you'd like to read along, please do! Or you can simply listen as I read God's words.

Philippians 4:6 says, "Pray about everything. Tell God what you need, and thank him for all he has done."

Let's practice doing what this verse says right now. We'll silently pray and tell God how we're feeling today. After our thinking prayer, we'll pray a special prayer all together.

Invite kids to get comfortable and close their eyes as they pray.

Pray: Dear God, we want to tell you how we feel today and why we feel that way. Pause for several moments of silent prayer. **Thanks for listening, God.**

Say: Now let's pray all together. We'll ask God to guide our time together today.

Watch and do what I do! After each sentence, I'll pause and we'll say the words "All together" together!

Pray: Dear God,

> **May we love** [make the shape of a heart with your hands] **you and each other.** ("All together!")
>
> **May we listen** [cup hand behind ear] **to you and each other.** ("All together!")
>
> **May we learn** [point to brain] **about you and each other.** ("All together!")
>
> **May we laugh and have fun** [high-five a friend] **with you and each other.** ("All together!")
>
> **Thanks for bringing us** ("All together!") **today. Amen.**

Supplies:
- Feelings Charts (1 for every 2 kids)
- crayons

Download and print or make one copy of the Feelings Chart on page 9 for every two people. Instead of printing each week, consider placing the charts in plastic sheet protectors. Then kids can use dry-erase markers to mark how they're feeling. Simply clean off the markings for next week!

This prayer will set the tone for your time together each lesson. Each sentence helps to communicate the values in your classroom and invites God to help everyone do their part, no matter their age! When behavior challenges arise, you can guide kids back to this prayer, to steer them toward loving behaviors.

Lesson 4

📖 Bible Discovery (15 minutes)

Find and read a verse together, explore its Bible context, and talk about stories in the Bible that reinforce the main idea of the verse.

Supplies:
- Bible bookmarked at Psalm 23:1
- chenille wires (several per child)
- child-safe scissors

Find and read Psalm 23:1.

Say: Let's hear a Bible verse that'll help us get to know God even better. Today we'll explore Psalm 23:1.

The Bible is one book made up of separate *books* that have *chapters* and *verses*. Let's hear Psalm 23:1. "Psalm" is the book, "23" is the chapter, and "1" is the verse. Many people really love the whole chapter of Psalm 23. Let's start with the first verse for now, then we'll hear the rest later.

Invite the Ready Reader to read the verse from your marked Bible. After the verse is read, have everyone tap their feet on the floor to thank the Ready Reader for reading.

Ask: What does this verse tell us about God?

Say: God is our shepherd. A shepherd takes care of sheep, making sure they have what they need and that they stay out of trouble. Just for fun, have kids make happy sheep "baas" because they have a good shepherd.

Now, we aren't really sheep—we're people! Still, the words of Psalm 23 describe what it's like for people to be cared for by God. God takes care of us. *(It's true!)*

That's our Bible Point today. So every time you hear the words "God takes care of us," give two thumbs up and say, "It's true!" To practice, repeat the Bible Point and response several times.

Shape chenille wires into objects to tell about David.

This verse is part of a longer poem written by a man named David. David was an important person in God's story that we read in the Bible. God picked David to be king over his people, called the Israelites. Let's make a crown to wear as we hear more about David.

Make chenille wires available, and encourage each child to cut and twist some wires into a crown to wear. Encourage Happy Helpers to offer to help younger children cut and twist the wires. (You may need to offer assistance too!)

David may have been king, but he knew *God* was really the one in charge. David's heart loved and trusted God. As you make your crown, listen to what David wrote in Psalm 23.

📖 Read aloud Psalm 23. Then invite everyone to wear their crowns.

Nice crowns, everyone! Before David was king, he was a shepherd. He wrote those beautiful words about God that we just heard. Since David was a shepherd, let's turn our crowns into something new. Now let's each make a shepherd's staff. Use a chenille wire to show everyone the basic shape of a shepherd's staff.

Ask: Why might someone use a staff or a cane today? How does it help them? Invite ideas from the group.

Say: A cane helps support people as they walk. It helps protect them from falling. Having something strong and sturdy nearby makes a big difference! In a similar way, shepherds used staffs to help them walk up steep hills. They used them to guide sheep in the right direction and to protect sheep when danger was nearby.

Ask: How is friendship with God like a shepherd's staff? Invite responses from the whole group.

Have everyone hold up their chenille-wire staffs. **Say: God is a friend we can depend on. God gives us the support we need to keep trusting and following him. Like a shepherd with his staff cares for his sheep, God cares for his people!**

David knew what to do with a shepherd's staff—because he was a shepherd! David was in charge of watching his dad's sheep. I guess it was like one of his chores.

Ask: What chores do you do at home?

Say: Maybe you take care of a pet at your house. Well, David had to shepherd and guide *all* his family's sheep.

Hear how God took care of David during scary times.

One day, David's dad asked him to take some food to his brothers who were part of the army. You see, God's people faced terrible enemies called the Philistines. One of the Philistine warriors was named Goliath. Goliath was big and strong, and he said terrible things about God's people. Let's make a Goliath with our chenille wires.

Have everyone work together to make a tall stick figure with their chenille wires.

David remembered when God had been with him during tough times as a shepherd, and he trusted that God would take care of him again. So David volunteered to fight Goliath! Listen to what he told King Saul.

Read aloud 1 Samuel 17:32-37.

God had helped David the shepherd fight off lions and bears, oh my! And David trusted that God would take care of him as he fought Goliath, too.

Lesson 4   51

Sure enough, God helped David defeat his enemy, Goliath! Bye-bye, Goliath! Have kids disassemble the chenille-wire man. **God took care of David, and God takes care of us. Listen to this part of Psalm 23.**

Read aloud Psalm 23:4.

God is our shepherd, even when things are scary. David didn't leave his sheep alone when the lion and bear came, and God doesn't leave his people all alone, either. Let's connect our wires into the shape of a heart now to help us remember that God takes care of us. *(It's true!)* Work together to shape everyone's chenille wires into one large heart.

Pray together.

From humble shepherd to mighty king, David's life was pretty cool! But the thing he was most known for was being a man who loved and trusted God. All throughout David's life, God took care of David's needs. And we can trust that God cares for our needs, too.

I wonder, what do you need today? Maybe you need God to support you as you do your chores. Or maybe you need God's help when friends aren't very kind to you.

Ask: What do you need from God today? Share a kid-friendly example from your life, then welcome anyone who wants to share with the group.

Say: Since we don't have sturdy shepherd's staffs to lean on, let's all stand and lean on a chair or a wall as we tell God about our needs. Allow time for kids to find a good leaning spot.

I'll pray and talk to God, our good shepherd, as we lean. Prayer person, be ready to end our prayer.

Pray: Dear God, as we lean on things in this room, we think about how strong and supportive you are. You are our shepherd who takes such good care of us. Pray specifically for needs kids mentioned and other needs in your church that you know about. **May we always lean on you when we need care and support. In Jesus' name.**

Ask the Prayer Person to pray a simple prayer or simply say "Amen!"

Wonder What Stations (15-20 minutes)

Kids will wonder and wander their way through these three free-flowing application activities. Young kids may gravitate toward some things while older kids are drawn to others.

Say: Let's keep exploring Psalm 23:1 with the items in this Wonder What Bin. You'll have three choices—I wonder what you'll choose to do first!

Dramatically re-reveal what's inside the Wonder What Bin, and explain these three different options for kids to choose during a free-play time. After 15-20 minutes, tell kids you'll be cleaning up the Wonder What Stations in about a minute. Have Happy Helpers return supplies to the Wonder What Bin.

Supplies:
- Wonder What Bin

Create

Draw a squiggly, wiggly path on a piece of paper. Then place the paper in a bag and seal it. Use a straw to place a drop of water on the page, then gently blow through the straw to guide the water droplet along the path.

Ask: What did you learn as you guided the water droplet along the path?

Say: Perhaps you realized that you needed to gently guide the water. Or maybe you saw that you had to take a deeper breath. Guiding something isn't always easy. But we have a good guide who always takes care of us. It's God! God takes care of us. *(It's true!)*

Let's Play

Play board games.

Ask: How does this game remind you of God shepherding or guiding people through life?

Say: Board games are fun—but you never know what'll happen! Our lives may have lots of twists, turns, and unexpected disappointment. But through it all, God takes care of us. *(It's true!)*

As kids play, meander around the area, using these questions and comments to connect each activity to today's Bible verse and Bible Point.

Try This

Try to keep the beach ball from hitting the ground. Work together to safely guide it across the room and back.

Ask: What happened when the beach ball fell and hit the ground?

How does God take care of people when they feel down?

Say: God takes care of us. *(It's true!)* **When we feel happy and when we feel down, God never changes. We can trust that he will give us what we need no matter how we feel.**

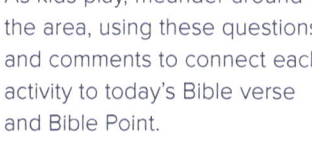

Lesson 4

Review Together (5 minutes)

> Explore a Jesus Connection and work together to create actions for words in the Bible verse.

Supplies:
- Here & Home papers (1 per child)
- crayons

Say: When God is our shepherd, we have everything we need. We have love and strength. And through Jesus, we have hope and a forever friend!

Let's create some actions to do as we say Psalm 23:1 all together. Rather than *me* telling you what to do, you kids can create the actions for us. You're in charge!

Invite kids to work together to make up actions for these words:
- the Lord
- everything
- need

Say Psalm 23:1 together with actions:
"The Lord is my shepherd; I have all that I need."

God takes such good care of his children. In good times and bad times, we can trust that God is with us and will give us the strength we need. God takes care of us. *(It's true!)* **And I trust that God will lead and guide you this week.**

Take some time to bless kids by name, asking God to take good care of them this week.

Here & Home

Give kids each the Here & Home paper on page 55. Invite them to color and complete the Bible verse page now, and point out the activity for them to lead their parents in at home.

God Takes Care of Us

Here

In Psalm 23, David describes a happy place with "green meadows" and "quiet streams." Add some color to David's happy place, drawing additional flowers, sheep, or other things David may have seen in a meadow. As you do, tell a friend about a place that makes you happy.

"The Lord is my shepherd; I have all that I need."
Psalm 23:1

Home

God Takes Care of Us

"The Lord is my shepherd; I have all that I need" (Psalm 23:1).

It's a beautiful poem. Its words paint vivid pictures of the mountains and valleys people encounter in life. It has inspired books. It's read at church services. It's recalled from memory in the dark of night. It's Psalm 23.

Pause with your family and read it now. (If you have readers in your family, let them have a turn too!)

"The Lord is my shepherd; I have all that I need.
He lets me rest in green meadows; he leads me beside peaceful streams.
He renews my strength.
He guides me along right paths, bringing honor to his name.
Even when I walk through the darkest valley, I will not be afraid, for you are close beside me. Your rod and your staff protect and comfort me.
You prepare a feast for me in the presence of my enemies.
You honor me by anointing my head with oil. My cup overflows with blessings.
Surely your goodness and unfailing love will pursue me all the days of my life, and I will live in the house of the Lord forever."
(Psalm 23)

Fun Fact

According to the *Wycliff Bible Encyclopedia*, the shepherd's staff in Psalm 23 represents "security, protection, and perhaps the nearness of God." What object in your life reminds you of God's nearness in a similar way?

_____

Think & Talk

What's your favorite part of this psalm? Why do you like that part?

Read & Do

This week, read this psalm each night at bedtime. Think of different things to do as you read. You could have one person read a line, and let everyone else repeat after them. You could whisper-read it. You could draw a picture to show the different things in the verse. You could look for pictures online that remind you of different parts of the verse.

Say & Pray

Tell God some of the things your family needs right now. Then pray, "Lord, you are our shepherd. Thanks for giving us all we need."

Lesson 4　57

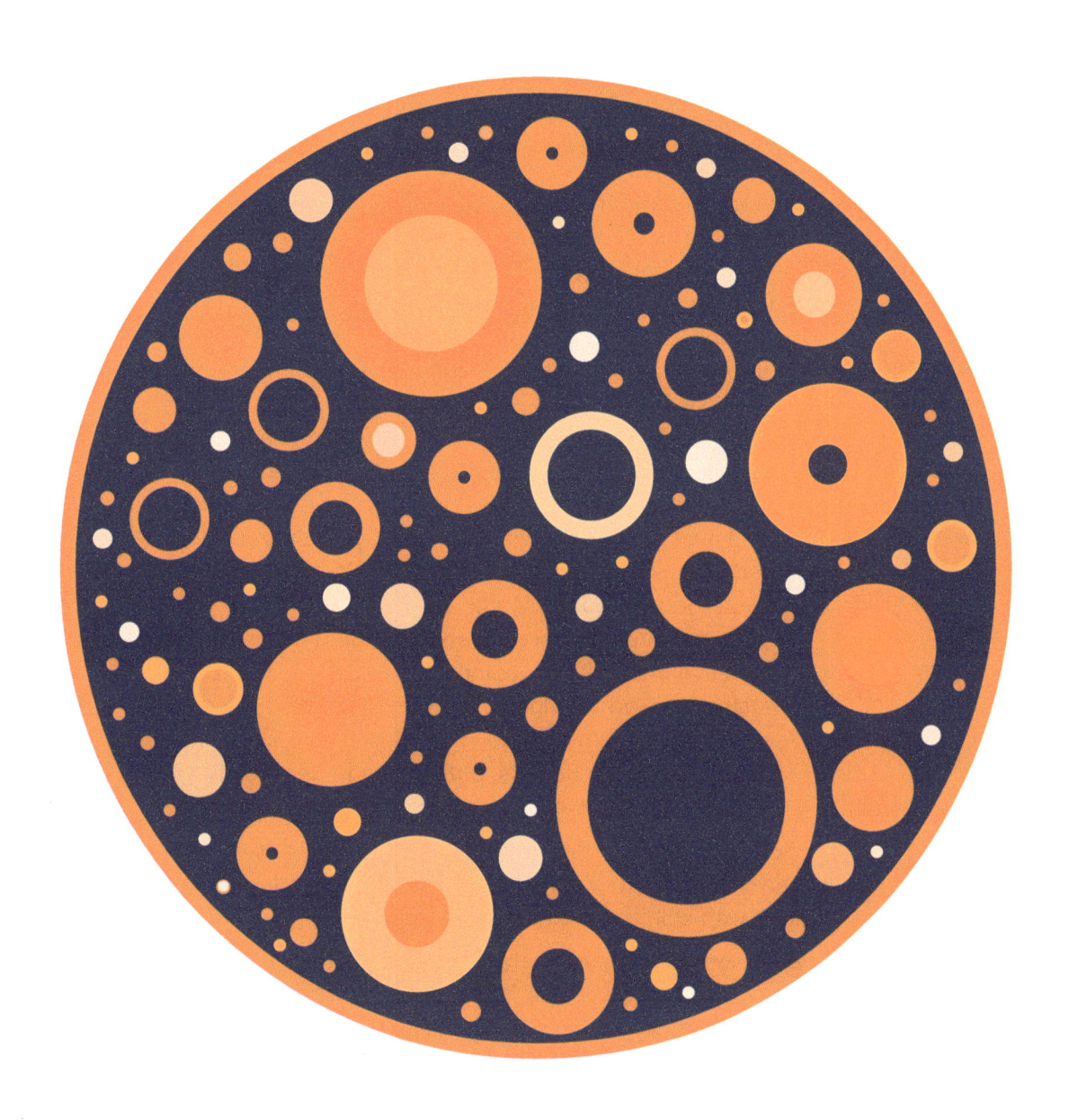

Lesson 5

God Is in Charge

"Be still, and know that I am God!" (Psalm 46:10)

Fun Fact

The Egyptians' chariots would have been high-tech weapons in the ancient Near East. Having seen them coming, the Israelites may have wondered how they'd ever fight back. But even the most high-tech weapons are no match for the one true God.

Discover Psalm 46:10

Leadership sounds fun, right? The titles "line leader," "team captain," "manager," and "chief executive officer" sure sound appealing.

But then you have to walk to a new place you've never been to before. Or your team loses the big game. Then the store's fire alarms won't stop bleating, or your company files for bankruptcy. Do you want to be in charge then?

Let's face it—being in charge is a lot of responsibility. We can go, go, go trying to prove that we have everything under control, or we can look to Psalm 46:10 for advice:

"Be still, and know that I am God!" God is in charge.

Having left slavery in Egypt, the Israelites may have been ready to take the reins and call the shots. But then they found themselves stuck between a lot of water and a lot of mighty chariots. What would they do? Moses' words reminded them who would fight for them: "Just stand still and watch the Lord rescue you today" (Exodus 14:13).

So, teacher, are you nervous about leading this lesson? Nervous about handling situations that may come your way? God is in charge. Simply be still and watch what God will do...

- as you have fun and play with kids.
- as you model kindness, patience, and generosity.
- as you help kids grow in relationship with God and each other.

So before the kids arrive, the noise level increases, and the fun begins, be still. Remember that God is God. Trust that God will work through you to share his love with children today.

PRAYER

Dear God, I still my body, my mind, and my heart so I can focus on you. You lead me so well. Guide this lesson today. Amen.

Lesson Overview

✝ **Bible Verse:** Psalm 46:10 | **Bible Point:** God is in charge. *(It's true!)* | **Bible Exploration:** Exodus 14; Psalm 46

Lesson-at-a-Glance

Play Together (10-15 minutes)
Line up and knock over dominoes and/or see how long kids can sit perfectly still.

Talk Together | Pray Together (10 minutes)
Talk about how you're feeling today, then pray and talk with God about it.

Bible Discovery (10-15 minutes)
Find and read Psalm 46:10 together, use shaving cream to re-create the story of how God helped the Israelites cross the Red Sea, and talk about troubles kids are facing today.

Wonder What Stations (15-20 minutes)
Choose and move through the following activities:

- Take a Look: Read and look through Bible story books and classic children's books, noticing who was in charge in the stories and who needed help.
- Imagine That: Play Freeze Dance as kids imagine they're the Israelites crossing the Red Sea with God's help.
- Let's Play: Play a counting game with dominoes and think about how God is in charge of math and other school subjects.

Review Together (5 minutes)
Explore a Jesus Connection, work together to create actions for words in the Bible verse, and give out Here & Home papers.

Supply List

- ☐ Bible bookmarked at Psalm 46:10
- ☐ All Together Tasks labels (1 sheet for every 8 kids) (on page 8)
- ☐ Feelings Charts (1 for every 2 kids) (on page 9)
- ☐ table
- ☐ shaving cream
- ☐ paper towels
- ☐ Here & Home papers (1 per child) (on page 67)
- ☐ crayons

Wonder What Bin Contents

- ☐ dominoes
- ☐ Bible storybooks and classic children's storybooks like *Curious George*
- ☐ upbeat music and music player

The "Wonder What Bin"

This supply box is a key part of each All Together Sunday School lesson. This large container will store all the toys and supplies needed for the Play Together activities and Wonder What Stations. Each week, kids will "wonder what" is in store for them! Your Wonder What Bin could be a plastic storage bin, a treasure chest, a toy box, or any large container.

All Together Tasks

Supplies: All Together Tasks labels (1 sheet for every 8 kids)

As kids arrive, explain the special jobs and encourage each child to choose one to do today. Download and print the All Together Tasks labels or copy them from page 8, and let kids choose the jobs they want to do. It's okay if more than one child has the same job or if one child has a few jobs. Teachers can have another job, too!

Kids choose from the following jobs:

Ready Reader is ready and willing to read a Bible verse aloud.

Prayer Person prays aloud nice and loud so everyone can hear.

Happy Helpers jump at the chance to hand out supplies and clean up stuff.

Befrienders are on the lookout for those who need help and support.

Greeters say, "Hello and welcome!" to everyone as they arrive and "Have a good day!" to everyone as they leave.

Play Together (10-15 minutes)

Play with the kids, using their favorite toys and games to help introduce the Bible Point. Choose one or both activities.

Supplies:
- Wonder What Bin

Dominoes

Work together to line up dominoes in a row, then push over the first domino and see if they all fall down. Then set them up again so they go in a circle or zigzag.

Ask: What made all the dominoes fall down?

Say: Only one domino had to move. The rest simply stayed still and waited to move. You know, it can be hard to stay still and wait for something to happen. But when we trust that <u>God is in charge</u>, he'll help us wait for him to act!

Ask: Tell about a time it was hard for you to be still when you were waiting for something to happen.

Stay Still

How long can you sit perfectly still? Have someone count to 10 while everyone else tries to sit completely still. Then have everyone stand and stay still for 20 seconds. Play again, changing positions and time each round. You could sit, stand, crouch, plank, or stand on tiptoes.

Ask: Tell about a time you had to be really still. What was it like?

Say: Today we'll hear about a time in the Bible when God's people were in a scary situation. Instead of fighting or running, their leader told them to "stand still and watch the Lord rescue you today." The people found out that <u>God is in charge</u>.

Talk Together (5 minutes)

> Kids talk in pairs about how they're feeling today.

Say: Today we'll talk with God and hear what God has to say to us as we read and explore the Bible. But first, let's talk to each other. Sometimes it's good to just sit still and talk with a friend about what's going on in your life and how you're feeling about it. Let's do that now!

Form pairs, and give each pair a Feelings Chart and a crayon. Have partners each circle the face that reflects how they're feeling in this moment and then tell their partners why they chose that face. Be sure to find a partner, too, and participate with the kids as they chat.

Supplies:
- Feelings Charts (1 for every 2 kids)
- crayons

Download and print or make one copy of the Feelings Chart on page 9 for every two people. Instead of printing each week, consider placing the charts in plastic sheet protectors. Then kids can use dry-erase markers to mark how they're feeling. Simply clean off the markings for next week!

Pray Together (5 minutes)

> Kids tell God how they're feeling and pray a prayer all together.

Say: Feelings change based on what's happening around us. But God's love for us never changes. We can pray and tell God about anything—even our feelings! Philippians 4:6 says, "Pray about everything. Tell God what you need, and thank him for all he has done."

Like we just talked with our friends, we can talk with God. God hears our prayers—no matter how loud they are. So just for fun, let's all whisper a prayer to God.

Invite kids to get comfortable and close their eyes as they pray.

Pray: Dear God, we want to tell you how we feel today and why we feel that way. This is how we feel today. Invite kids to whisper how they feel. **Thanks for listening, God, and for loving us no matter how we feel.**

Say: Now let's ask God to guide our time together today. Watch and do what I do! After each sentence, I'll pause and we'll whisper the words "All together" together!

Pray: Dear God,
May we love [make the shape of a heart with your hands] **you and each other.** ("All together!")

May we listen [cup hand behind ear] **to you and each other.** ("All together!")

May we learn [point to brain] **about you and each other.** ("All together!")

May we laugh and have fun [high-five a friend] **with you and each other.** ("All together!")

Thanks for bringing us ("All together!") **today. Amen.**

This prayer will set the tone for your time together each lesson. Each sentence helps to communicate the values in your classroom and invites God to help everyone do their part, no matter their age! When behavior challenges arise, you can guide kids back to this prayer, to steer them toward loving behaviors.

📖 Bible Discovery (15 minutes)

Find and read a verse together, explore its Bible context, and talk about stories in the Bible that reinforce the main idea of the verse.

Supplies:
- Bible bookmarked at Psalm 46:10
- table
- shaving cream
- paper towels

Find and read Psalm 46:10.

Say: Let's hear a Bible verse that'll help us learn to trust God even more. Today we'll explore Psalm 46:10. God inspired different people to write down just what he wanted to say. We read those words in the Bible!

Let's hear Psalm 46:10. "Psalms" is the name of the Bible book. The book of Psalms is filled with a bunch of different psalms, or songs! So Psalm, chapter 46, verse 10 is part of a song written to praise God.

Invite the Ready Reader to read the verse from your marked Bible. Have everyone clap to thank the Ready Reader for reading.

Ask: What does this verse tell us about God?

Say: This verse tells us we don't need to fight back or make things happen on our own. We can be still and trust that <u>God is in charge</u>.

That's our Bible Point today. So every time you hear the words "God is in charge," give two thumbs up and say, "It's true!" To practice, repeat the Bible Point and response several times.

Let's read another verse in this psalm.

📖 Read Psalm 46:1.

A *refuge* is a safe place. God is our safe place! We can trust that God is ready to help us in times of trouble.

God helped a group of people called the Israelites when they faced tough stuff. We read about the Israelites in the Bible.

The Israelites were forced to be slaves in a place called Egypt. But God rescued them from those troubles. God gave them leaders named Moses and Aaron and Miriam who guided them away from Egypt and toward the new home God promised to give them. God was in charge of the Israelites and took good care of them.

Use shaving cream to tell the story of how God helped the Israelites cross the Red Sea.

Let's explore the story of how God helped the Israelites escape from the Egyptians. We'll use shaving cream to help us!

Have kids sit or stand around a table. Make sure nothing is on the table as you begin the story.

This story comes from the Bible book of Exodus. Show the shaving cream, and remind kids it's like soap—not like whipped cream. (No eating—blech!) Give everyone a dollop of shaving cream. Have kids choose one hand

62 All Together Sunday School Book 1

to smooth it in front of them, like a page. Tell them they'll use the other, clean hand to draw in the shaving cream.

God had helped the Israelites move away from hard times in Egypt. That made them happy. Have kids use one hand to smooth out the shaving cream. Have them use the other, clean hand to draw a happy face.

But the leader of Egypt, called Pharaoh, didn't like that the Israelites had left. Have kids smooth out the shaving cream and then draw a mad face.

So Pharaoh commanded his army to chase after them. Back then, the Egyptians had horses and chariots in their army. Chariots are fancy wagons. We may think that wagons or chariots are old ways to travel now, but back then, they were brand new! Have kids smooth out the shaving cream and then draw a horse and chariot.

When the Israelites saw the Egyptian army with horses and chariots coming after them, they were scared! Terrified even! But Moses reminded the people that God is in charge. Listen to what he said.

Read Exodus 14:13-14.

Everyone be still! Don't touch the shaving cream or the table. Can you stay completely still for 30 seconds?

Ask: **What was it like to stay still, and not touch anything?**

Say: **It's hard to stay still! When there is a big mess or we're in big trouble, it's hard not to run away and avoid the problem.**

Remember Psalm 46:10? When troubles come, God has words for us. He says, "Be still, and know that I am God." When things are messy, we can trust that God is in charge and God will do something to help us. We have to trust him!

Ask: **Why can it be hard to trust God?** Share an example from your own life to start the conversation.

Say: **Even though we can't see God, we can trust that God is with us and <u>God is in charge</u>.** *(It's true!)* **I'll give you a paper towel now to remind you of that truth.** Give each child a full-size paper towel. As you do, say: [Child's name], **<u>God is in charge</u>.** *(It's true!)* Invite kids to wipe off their hands with the paper towels. Then they'll keep the paper towels to use for the next part of the story.

On their way out of Egypt, the Israelites had stopped beside some water called the Red Sea. Imagine your shaving cream is the Red Sea. The Israelites needed to get across the sea and away from the Egyptian chariots and horses!

God told Moses to reach out his hand. Have everyone reach out the hand that's holding the paper towel. **Let's read what happened next.**

Read Exodus 14:21-22.

Let's use the paper towels to make a path right through the shaving cream! Then walk your fingers down the dry path like they're people! Allow time.

The Israelites were safe! They didn't have to fix the problem on their own. God was in charge. (It's true!) **God twisted the wheels on the Egyptians' chariots so they couldn't roll very well. And once the Israelites were all safe and sound, God made the water return and cover up all the chariots. It was scary! But God was in charge.** (It's true!)

Invite kids to use their hands to cover up the path again and then keep rubbing the shaving cream until it disappears or use more paper towels to clean the table and kids' hands.

Pray together.

God's in charge today, too. (It's true!) **Let's be still and think about a question together.**

Ask: **What troubles have you been facing?** Share an example from your own life to start the conversation.

Say: **Chariots might not be chasing you, but maybe a friend or brother or sister says hurtful words sometimes. Or maybe you have a sea of worry that's filling up your mind and heart.**

You may not be able to make that trouble go away. But *you* don't have to! You aren't in charge. God is! We can be still and know that God is in charge. (It's true!) **Let's be still as we pray and talk with God now.** Invite kids to find a comfortable position and be still. **Prayer Person, will you talk with God for us to end the prayer? I'll give you a signal when it's time.**

Pray: **Dear God, you know the troubles we face. May we be still and know that you are God. Thanks for being in charge. You are more powerful than anything. May we trust that you are with us and that you care. In Jesus' name, amen.**

Wonder What Stations (15-20 minutes)

> Kids will wonder and wander their way through these three free-flowing application activities. Young kids may gravitate toward some things while older kids are drawn to others.

Say: Let's keep exploring Psalm 46:10 with the items in this Wonder What Bin. You'll have three choices—I wonder what you'll choose to do first!

Dramatically re-reveal what's inside the Wonder What Bin, and explain these three different options for kids to choose during a free-play time. After 15-20 minutes, tell kids you'll be cleaning up the Wonder What Stations in about a minute. Have Happy Helpers return supplies to the Wonder What Bin.

Supplies:
- Wonder What Bin

Take a Look

Invite older kids to read books with younger kids. Or allow kids to browse books independently.

Ask: Who needed help in the story you read?

Ask: Who was in charge?

Say: We people tend to get ourselves into some tricky situations sometimes. And it's hard to find a way out on our own. Thankfully, <u>God is in charge</u>. *(It's true!)* We can be still and trust that God is a loving father who cares for us.

Imagine That

Imagine you are the Israelites moving toward the Promised Land. Walk, jog, or march in place while the music plays, and be still when it stops! Say Psalm 46:10 together while everyone is "frozen." Then resume the music again.

Ask: **Tell about a time you enjoyed being still.** Share an example from your own life to start the conversation.

Say: Being still isn't so bad after all! When we are still, we can rest, catch our breath, and remember that <u>God is in charge</u>. *(It's true!)*

As kids play, meander around the area, using these questions and comments to connect each activity to today's Bible verse and Bible Point.

Let's Play

Lay out the dominoes face up. Choose one person to call out a number between 1 and 12. Whoever grabs a domino with that many dots first wins and calls out the next number.

Say: We had to count and use math to play this game. Did you know that God is even in charge of math? <u>God is in charge</u> of everything—including math and science and other things we learn about in school. *(It's true!)* It's so cool to think that the God who created everything loves and cares for us.

Ask: What do you like to learn about? Math? Science? History? God's in charge of it all!

Lesson 5   65

Review Together (5 minutes)

Explore a Jesus Connection and work together to create actions for words in the Bible verse.

Supplies:
- Here & Home papers (1 per child)
- crayons

Say: God rescued the Israelites from Egypt. And God still rescues people today! God sent his special Son, Jesus, to save people from sin.

Sin causes us to think we are in charge instead of God. Sin gets everyone in trouble. But <u>God is in charge</u> *(It's true!)*, so he sent Jesus to help us with our sin problem and make a way for us to be close to God forever! We don't earn or work for God's friendship. We can simply be still and know that God is in charge.

Let's create some actions to do as we say Psalm 46:10 all together. Rather than *me* telling you what to do, you kids are in charge! Will you create the actions for us?

Invite kids to work together to make up actions for these words:

- still
- know
- I am God

Say Psalm 46:10 together with actions:
"Be still, and know that I am God!"

<u>God is in charge</u>. *(It's true!)* **So when troubles come, we can be still and talk to God about them. God will help us know what and *what not* to do!**

Take some time to bless kids by name, reminding them that God is in charge of each part of their day today.

Here & Home

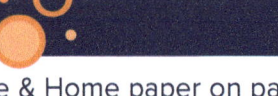

Give kids each the Here & Home paper on page 67. Invite them to color and complete the Bible verse page now, and point out the activity for them to lead their parents in at home.

---

66   All Together Sunday School Book 1

God Is in Charge

Here

Color this picture with a friend. One person will hold the crayon but keep their arm still. The other person will guide their friend's hand, moving it so it colors! Trade roles so each friend has a turn holding the crayon. How is a friend helping you color like God helping us?

"Be still, and know that I am God!"
Psalm 46:10

Home

God Is in Charge

"Be still, and know that I am God!" (Psalm 46:10)

Leadership sounds fun, right? The titles "line leader," "team captain," "manager," and "chief executive officer" sure sound appealing.

But then you have to walk to a new place you've never been to before. Or your team loses the big game. Then the store's fire alarms won't stop bleating, or your company files for bankruptcy. Do you want to be in charge then?

Let's face it—being in charge is a lot of responsibility. We can go, go, go trying to prove that we have everything under control, or we can look to Psalm 46:10 for advice:

"Be still, and know that I am God!" God is in charge.

Having left slavery in Egypt, the Israelites may have been ready to take the reins and call the shots. But then they found themselves stuck between a lot of water and a lot of mighty chariots. What would they do? Moses' words reminded them who would fight for them: "Just stand still and watch the Lord rescue you today" (Exodus 14:13).

When you feel stuck, or under attack, you don't need to lead a charge of revenge. God's in charge. You can be still and trust that God cares for you and will help you.

Fun Fact

The Egyptians' chariots would have been high-tech weapons in the ancient Near East. Having seen them coming, the Israelites may have wondered how they'd ever fight back. But even the most high-tech weapons are no match for the one true God.

Think & Talk

Do you like being in charge of things? Why or why not?

Read & Do

Read Exodus 14:13-14. Then pretend your kitchen sink is the Red Sea. What could you float on the water to create a path through the water?

It's a good thing we weren't in charge of saving the Israelites. God's solution was much better.

Say & Pray

After you're tucked in bed and you're cozy and still, think back on all the things that happened today—good stuff and not-so-good stuff. Thank God for being in charge.

Lesson 5

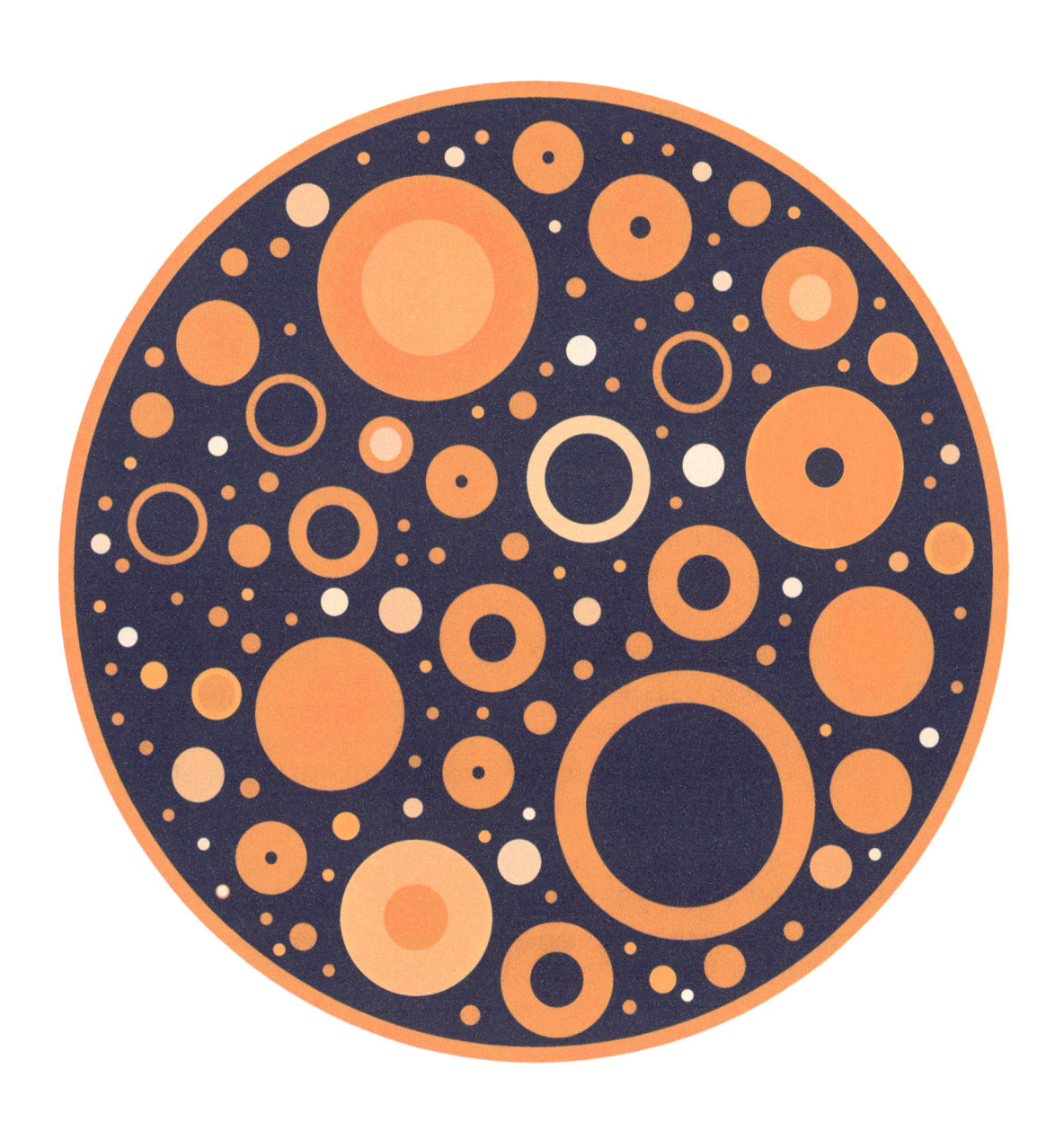

Lesson 6

God Gives Us Hope

" 'For I know the plans I have for you,' says the Lord. 'They are plans for good and not for disaster, to give you a future and a hope' " (Jeremiah 29:11).

Discover Jeremiah 29:11

The words of Jeremiah 29:11 speak to people living in hopeless exile. Jeremiah did not address his letter "Dear 21st Century Christian." Rather, he wrote to a specific group of people—the Judean exiles living in Babylon after the fall of Jerusalem. Families whose plans had been altered by tragedy. A community whose hopes had been smashed with Jerusalem's walls.

Remembering this context can bring fresh richness to this often-referred-to verse. It's not a go-to reminder to "hang in there" but a promise from God that he sees *you*, and his plans for your life are rooted in his love for you.

As you read these words from God today, it's okay to acknowledge your own mangled plans and hopeless longings. The God who had hope and a future for the exiles in Babylon still offers hope and a future for his children today—including the children you lead.

God gives us hope. When things in kids' lives don't go as they planned or imagined, hope from God remains.

- When kids navigate changes in plans, God gives them hope.
- When kids struggle to identify and work through feelings, God gives them hope.
- When kids wonder about heaven and what happens to people who love Jesus, God gives them hope.

The hope God gives comforts kids' hearts and reminds them to trust that God has good things in store for them—today and for eternity.

PRAYER

Dear God, I trust that you have good plans for me and for all your children. May I find my hope in you today. In Jesus' name, amen.

Fun Fact

The last king of Judah was Zedekiah. He was 21 years old when he became king. He was stubborn and refused to turn back to God, and, well…things didn't turn out so well for him. Read all about it in 2 Kings 24:18–25:7.

Lesson Overview

Bible Verse: Jeremiah 29:11 | **Bible Point:** God gives us hope. *(It's true!)* | **Bible Exploration:** Jeremiah 29:11; 2 Chronicles 36:18-21

Lesson-at-a-Glance

Play Together (10-15 minutes)
Play Uno and think about what you hope happens in the game and/or play a name game where you try to remember things friends hope for.

Talk Together | Pray Together (10 minutes)
Talk about how you're feeling today, then pray and talk with God about it.

Bible Discovery (10-15 minutes)
Find and read Jeremiah 29:11 together, find out what *repent* means, and move to a new place in the room to explore what it's like to be in exile.

Wonder What Stations (15-20 minutes)
Choose and move through the following activities:
- **Imagine That:** Build Lego homes for God's people living in Babylon and talk about a home you'd want to settle into.
- **Let's Play:** Play Keep Away and talk about how God helps us find hope during tough times.
- **Create:** Make a Memory Game to play together and talk about things that help us remember that God gives us hope.

Review Together (5 minutes)
Explore a Jesus Connection, work together to create actions for words in the Bible verse, and give out Here & Home papers.

Supply List

- ☐ Bible bookmarked at Jeremiah 29:11
- ☐ All Together Tasks labels (1 sheet for every 8 kids) (on page 8)
- ☐ Feelings Charts (1 for every 2 kids) (on page 9)
- ☐ paper and pen or whiteboard and dry-erase marker
- ☐ clean trash can
- ☐ Here & Home papers (1 per child) (on page 79)
- ☐ crayons

Wonder What Bin Contents
- ☐ card games like Uno or Spot It!
- ☐ Legos or Duplo blocks
- ☐ playground ball
- ☐ index cards
- ☐ foam shape stickers

The "Wonder What Bin"

This supply box is a key part of each All Together Sunday School lesson. This large container will store all the toys and supplies needed for the Play Together activities and Wonder What Stations. Each week, kids will "wonder what" is in store for them! Your Wonder What Bin could be a plastic storage bin, a treasure chest, a toy box, or any large container.

All Together Tasks

Supplies: All Together Tasks labels (1 sheet for every 8 kids)

As kids arrive, explain the special jobs and encourage each child to choose one to do today. Download and print the All Together Tasks labels or copy them from page 8, and let kids choose the jobs they want to do. It's okay if more than one child has the same job or if one child has a few jobs. Teachers can have another job, too!

Kids choose from the following jobs:

Ready Reader is ready and willing to read a Bible verse aloud.

Prayer Person prays aloud nice and loud so everyone can hear.

Happy Helpers jump at the chance to hand out supplies and clean up stuff.

Befrienders are on the lookout for those who need help and support.

Greeters say, "Hello and welcome!" to everyone as they arrive and "Have a good day!" to everyone as they leave.

Play Together (10-15 minutes)

Play with the kids, using their favorite toys and games to help introduce the Bible Point. Choose one or both activities.

Supplies:
- Wonder What Bin

Uno Hope

Play a favorite card game like Uno or Spot It! Review the rules before playing so everyone knows what to do and can join the fun. Sporadically (and quietly) ask individuals what they hope will happen next.

Ask: How did your hopes for this game come true or not come true?

Say: As we play games, we hope certain things will happen so we can win! To have hope means that we trust something good will happen. Today we'll explore a Bible verse and find out that <u>God gives us hope</u>.

Hope Remembered

Form a circle or sit around a table together.

Ask: What's your name, and what's one hope you have for your next birthday?

The youngest person in the group will go first, answering the questions. The next person repeats what the first person said, then answers the questions too. Continue around the circle. Can the last people to go remember everyone's names and birthday hopes? Be ready to work together when needed.

Ask: What was it like trying to remember everyone's hopes?

Say: It may be hard for us to remember everyone's hopes for the future. But it's not hard for God! <u>God gives us hope</u>.

Talk Together (5 minutes)

> Kids talk in pairs about how they're feeling today.

Say: Today we'll talk with God and hear what God has to say to us through words in the Bible. I hope our time together will be fun and helpful to you as you grow to know God better. But first, let's talk together. **How are you feeling today?**

Form pairs, and give each pair a Feelings Chart and a crayon. Have partners each circle the face that reflects how they're feeling in this moment and then tell their partners why they chose that face. Be sure to find a partner, too, and participate with the kids as they chat.

Pray Together (5 minutes)

> Kids tell God how they're feeling and pray a prayer all together.

Say: Thanks for talking with a friend! In the Bible, we read that we can pray and tell God anything.

Philippians 4:6 says, "Pray about everything. Tell God what you need, and thank him for all he has done."

Like we just talked with our friends, we can talk with God! Let's practice doing that now! We'll silently pray and tell God how we're feeling today. We won't pray with our voices—instead we'll just think a prayer to God for a little bit. After our thinking prayer, we'll pray a special prayer all together.

Invite kids to get comfortable and close their eyes as they pray.

Pray: Dear God, we want to tell you how we feel today and why we feel that way. Pause for several moments of silent prayer. Thanks for listening, God.

Say: Now let's pray all together. We'll ask God to guide our time together today.

Watch and do what I do! After each sentence, I'll pause and we'll say the words "All together" together!

Pray: Dear God,

May we love [make the shape of a heart with your hands]
you and each other. ("All together!")

May we listen [cup hand behind ear]
to you and each other. ("All together!")

May we learn [point to brain]
about you and each other. ("All together!")

May we laugh and have fun [high-five a friend]
with you and each other. ("All together!")

Thanks for bringing us ("All together!") **today. Amen.**

Supplies:
- Feelings Charts (1 for every 2 kids)
- crayons

Download and print or make one copy of the Feelings Chart on page 9 for every two people. Instead of printing each week, consider placing the charts in plastic sheet protectors. Then kids can use dry-erase markers to mark how they're feeling. Simply clean off the markings for next week!

This prayer will set the tone for your time together each day. Each sentence helps to communicate the values in your classroom and invites God to help everyone do their part, no matter their age! When behavior challenges arise, you can guide kids back to this prayer to steer them toward loving behaviors.

📖 Bible Discovery (15 minutes)

Find and read a verse together, explore its Bible context, and talk about stories in the Bible that reinforce the main idea of the verse.

Supplies:
- Bible bookmarked at Jeremiah 29:11
- paper and pen or whiteboard and dry-erase marker
- container of Legos
- clean trash can

Find and read Jeremiah 29:11.

Say: Let's hear a Bible verse that'll help us get to know God even better. Today we'll explore Jeremiah 29:11.

The Bible book of Jeremiah is in the Old Testament of the Bible. It's named after a man named Jeremiah. Jeremiah was a prophet who told people messages from God. Let's hear Jeremiah 29:11. Jeremiah is the book, "29" is the chapter, and "11" is the verse.

Invite the Ready Reader to read the verse from your marked Bible. Have everyone clap to thank the Ready Reader for reading.

Ask: What does this verse tell us about God?

Say: This verse tells us that <u>God gives us hope</u>! That's our Bible Point today. So every time you hear the words "God gives us hope," give two thumbs up and say, "It's true!" To practice, repeat the Bible Point and response several times.

Plan how to build a city with Legos.

Jeremiah said these words to the people of Judah. They had once been known as the Israelites, God's special people. They lived in a place called Judah and had a great city called Jerusalem. There was a fancy palace for their king and a beautiful temple where people would go to honor God. It was like a dream come true!

Let's make a plan for how we can build Jerusalem with Legos. I'll make a list of what we'll do. Who has ideas for how we can make this awesome city? Invite ideas from kids, writing them on a piece of paper or a whiteboard.

I hope we have time to do all these things! What great plans!

Before we get started, I have to tell you: God's people had big plans, too. But then many of Judah's leaders ignored God. They thought they could keep things going great on their own. But they couldn't.

Jeremiah warned the people of Judah that they should repent. That means stop disobeying God and start following God again. When we repent, we turn from doing one thing and go another direction instead. I'll show you what I mean.

Learn what it means to repent.

Have everyone stand in the middle of your space. On "go," have them walk together toward one of the walls. When you say "Repent!" they should stop, turn around, and go the other direction. Play for a few minutes, then invite everyone to be seated again.

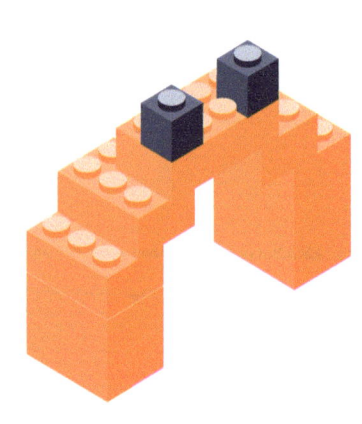

Jeremiah told God's people to repent or else something bad would happen: They'd lose their home in Judah. They'd lose Jerusalem, their palace, their temple, everything! People from another place called Babylon would come and take over.

Ask: **If a prophet like Jeremiah said you'd lose everything if you didn't change your behavior, would you repent? Why or why not?**

Say: **If we're doing something we know we shouldn't be doing, the fear of consequences or getting into trouble might make us stop what we're doing and do something else instead. Like if we know we won't get dessert, we might stop throwing peas across the kitchen.**

Experience exile.

Well, God's people did *not* change their behavior. So God's warning came true. The king of Babylon took over. His army hurt the people of Judah—even killed some of them! Babylon took stuff that was important to God's people. Take the container of Legos, and pour the Legos into a trash can. **It was awful. I'll read what happened.**

Read aloud 2 Chronicles 36:18-21.

Life was not happy or comfortable or safe for God's people anymore. Let's feel how they may have felt. No more sitting in our spots comfortably. Now we must stand. Have kids all stand, and have Happy Helpers help you stack chairs and put them away. Have everyone stand with you in a circle at a different spot in the room.

God's people were away from home in exile. *Exile* **is a word that means you have to leave and you can't come back. You would think that God was so mad that he'd just forget about the people of Judah and pick new people to love. But God didn't.**

Instead, God had words to share with his people. Those words are in the Bible verse we heard earlier, Jeremiah 29:11. Ready Reader, will you read it for us?

Have the Ready Reader read Jeremiah 29:11 aloud. Invite kids to stomp their feet seven times to thank the Ready Reader for reading.

This verse is part of a letter that God told Jeremiah to write for his people when they were in Babylon. At the beginning of the letter, God told them to get settled and make homes in Babylon. There was hope for a good life there. Life would go on as normal in this new place. They should get married and have children. Even if they had always planned to live in Jerusalem all their lives, now they should plan to be in Babylon and make the most of it.

So, friends, let's get comfortable. Instead of standing, let's lie down and plan to stay awhile. Invite kids to remain in a circle but lie on their tummies with heads propped up on elbows so they can still see each other and you.

Lesson 6   75

This is not what God's people planned. But God didn't leave them. Instead, God gave them hope. God wanted them to trust that good things were ahead. I'll read Jeremiah 29:11 again, and I'll read what God said after that verse, too.

Read aloud Jeremiah 29:11-14.

There was hope! God had good plans for his people, even if they looked different from what they expected. And someday, after 70 years, they'd get to go back to their home. Quickly count to 70 together, then have everyone scramble up, assist Happy Helpers in setting up chairs, and go back to their original seats.

Pray together.

These words written to God's people a *looong* time ago matter to us today, too. When things in our lives don't go as we hoped, <u>God gives us hope</u>. *(It's true!)*

When we hope, we look forward to good things. But they don't always have to be big, amazing things that may come someday. We can look forward to small, normal things that God brings us each day. If we watch for it, every day we'll spot ways <u>God gives us hope</u>. *(It's true!)*

Let's pray. Prayer Person, be ready to end our prayer with some simple words or just an "Amen!"

Dear God, we are sorry for times we don't obey you. We repent. Please forgive us and help us change our behavior. Jesus, thanks for the hope you give us. May we enjoy the hope you give us today even as we look forward to meeting you face-to-face someday.

Talk Together (5 minutes)

| Kids talk in pairs about how they're feeling today.

Say: Today we'll talk with God and hear what God has to say to us through words in the Bible. I hope our time together will be fun and helpful to you as you grow to know God better. But first, let's talk together. How are you feeling today?

Form pairs, and give each pair a Feelings Chart and a crayon. Have partners each circle the face that reflects how they're feeling in this moment and then tell their partners why they chose that face. Be sure to find a partner, too, and participate with the kids as they chat.

Pray Together (5 minutes)

| Kids tell God how they're feeling and pray a prayer all together.

Say: Thanks for talking with a friend! In the Bible, we read that we can pray and tell God anything.

Philippians 4:6 says, "Pray about everything. Tell God what you need, and thank him for all he has done."

Like we just talked with our friends, we can talk with God! Let's practice doing that now! We'll silently pray and tell God how we're feeling today. We won't pray with our voices—instead we'll just think a prayer to God for a little bit. After our thinking prayer, we'll pray a special prayer all together.

Invite kids to get comfortable and close their eyes as they pray.

Pray: Dear God, we want to tell you how we feel today and why we feel that way. Pause for several moments of silent prayer. **Thanks for listening, God.**

Say: Now let's pray all together. We'll ask God to guide our time together today.

Watch and do what I do! After each sentence, I'll pause and we'll say the words "All together" together!

Pray: Dear God,

> **May we love** [make the shape of a heart with your hands]
> **you and each other.** ("All together!")
>
> **May we listen** [cup hand behind ear]
> **to you and each other.** ("All together!")
>
> **May we learn** [point to brain]
> **about you and each other.** ("All together!")
>
> **May we laugh and have fun** [high-five a friend]
> **with you and each other.** ("All together!")
>
> **Thanks for bringing us** ("All together!") **today. Amen.**

Supplies:
- Feelings Charts (1 for every 2 kids)
- crayons

Download and print or make one copy of the Feelings Chart on page 9 for every two people. Instead of printing each week, consider placing the charts in plastic sheet protectors. Then kids can use dry-erase markers to mark how they're feeling. Simply clean off the markings for next week!

This prayer will set the tone for your time together each day. Each sentence helps to communicate the values in your classroom and invites God to help everyone do their part, no matter their age! When behavior challenges arise, you can guide kids back to this prayer to steer them toward loving behaviors.

📕 Bible Discovery (15 minutes)

Find and read a verse together, explore its Bible context, and talk about stories in the Bible that reinforce the main idea of the verse.

Supplies:
- Bible bookmarked at Jeremiah 29:11
- paper and pen or whiteboard and dry-erase marker
- container of Legos
- clean trash can

Find and read Jeremiah 29:11.

Say: Let's hear a Bible verse that'll help us get to know God even better. Today we'll explore Jeremiah 29:11.

The Bible book of Jeremiah is in the Old Testament of the Bible. It's named after a man named Jeremiah. Jeremiah was a prophet who told people messages from God. Let's hear Jeremiah 29:11. Jeremiah is the book, "29" is the chapter, and "11" is the verse.

Invite the Ready Reader to read the verse from your marked Bible. Have everyone clap to thank the Ready Reader for reading.

Ask: What does this verse tell us about God?

Say: This verse tells us that <u>God gives us hope</u>! That's our Bible Point today. So every time you hear the words "God gives us hope," give two thumbs up and say, "It's true!" To practice, repeat the Bible Point and response several times.

Plan how to build a city with Legos.

Jeremiah said these words to the people of Judah. They had once been known as the Israelites, God's special people. They lived in a place called Judah and had a great city called Jerusalem. There was a fancy palace for their king and a beautiful temple where people would go to honor God. It was like a dream come true!

Let's make a plan for how we can build Jerusalem with Legos. I'll make a list of what we'll do. Who has ideas for how we can make this awesome city? Invite ideas from kids, writing them on a piece of paper or a whiteboard.

I hope we have time to do all these things! What great plans!

Before we get started, I have to tell you: God's people had big plans, too. But then many of Judah's leaders ignored God. They thought they could keep things going great on their own. But they couldn't.

Jeremiah warned the people of Judah that they should repent. That means stop disobeying God and start following God again. When we repent, we turn from doing one thing and go another direction instead. I'll show you what I mean.

Learn what it means to repent.

Have everyone stand in the middle of your space. On "go," have them walk together toward one of the walls. When you say "Repent!" they should stop, turn around, and go the other direction. Play for a few minutes, then invite everyone to be seated again.

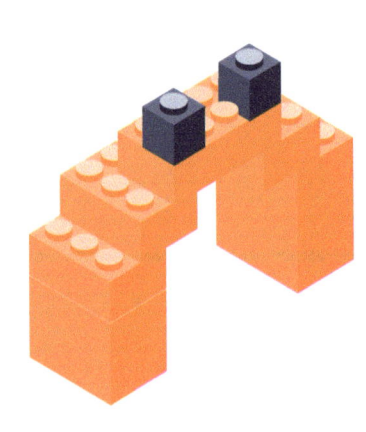

74 All Together Sunday School Book 1

Jeremiah told God's people to repent or else something bad would happen: They'd lose their home in Judah. They'd lose Jerusalem, their palace, their temple, everything! People from another place called Babylon would come and take over.

Ask: **If a prophet like Jeremiah said you'd lose everything if you didn't change your behavior, would you repent? Why or why not?**

Say: **If we're doing something we know we shouldn't be doing, the fear of consequences or getting into trouble might make us stop what we're doing and do something else instead. Like if we know we won't get dessert, we might stop throwing peas across the kitchen.**

Experience exile.

Well, God's people did *not* change their behavior. So God's warning came true. The king of Babylon took over. His army hurt the people of Judah—even killed some of them! Babylon took stuff that was important to God's people. Take the container of Legos, and pour the Legos into a trash can. **It was awful. I'll read what happened.**

Read aloud 2 Chronicles 36:18-21.

Life was not happy or comfortable or safe for God's people anymore. Let's feel how they may have felt. No more sitting in our spots comfortably. Now we must stand. Have kids all stand, and have Happy Helpers help you stack chairs and put them away. Have everyone stand with you in a circle at a different spot in the room.

God's people were away from home in exile. *Exile* is a word that means you have to leave and you can't come back. You would think that God was so mad that he'd just forget about the people of Judah and pick new people to love. But God didn't.

Instead, God had words to share with his people. Those words are in the Bible verse we heard earlier, Jeremiah 29:11. Ready Reader, will you read it for us?

Have the Ready Reader read Jeremiah 29:11 aloud. Invite kids to stomp their feet seven times to thank the Ready Reader for reading.

This verse is part of a letter that God told Jeremiah to write for his people when they were in Babylon. At the beginning of the letter, God told them to get settled and make homes in Babylon. There was hope for a good life there. Life would go on as normal in this new place. They should get married and have children. Even if they had always planned to live in Jerusalem all their lives, now they should plan to be in Babylon and make the most of it.

So, friends, let's get comfortable. Instead of standing, let's lie down and plan to stay awhile. Invite kids to remain in a circle but lie on their tummies with heads propped up on elbows so they can still see each other and you.

Lesson 6   75

This is not what God's people planned. But God didn't leave them. Instead, God gave them hope. God wanted them to trust that good things were ahead. I'll read Jeremiah 29:11 again, and I'll read what God said after that verse, too.

Read aloud Jeremiah 29:11-14.

There was hope! God had good plans for his people, even if they looked different from what they expected. And someday, after 70 years, they'd get to go back to their home. Quickly count to 70 together, then have everyone scramble up, assist Happy Helpers in setting up chairs, and go back to their original seats.

Pray together.

These words written to God's people a *looong* time ago matter to us today, too. When things in our lives don't go as we hoped, God gives us hope. *(It's true!)*

When we hope, we look forward to good things. But they don't always have to be big, amazing things that may come someday. We can look forward to small, normal things that God brings us each day. If we watch for it, every day we'll spot ways God gives us hope. *(It's true!)*

Let's pray. Prayer Person, be ready to end our prayer with some simple words or just an "Amen!"

Dear God, we are sorry for times we don't obey you. We repent. Please forgive us and help us change our behavior. Jesus, thanks for the hope you give us. May we enjoy the hope you give us today even as we look forward to meeting you face-to-face someday.

Wonder What Stations (15-20 minutes)

> Kids will wonder and wander their way through these three free-flowing application activities. Young kids may gravitate toward some things while older kids are drawn to others.

Say: Let's keep exploring Jeremiah 29:11 with the items in this Wonder What Bin. You'll have three choices—I wonder what you'll choose to do first!

Supplies:
- Wonder What Bin

Dramatically re-reveal what's inside the Wonder What Bin, and explain these three different options for kids to choose during a free-play time. After 15-20 minutes, tell kids you'll be cleaning up the Wonder What Stations in about a minute. Have Happy Helpers return supplies to the Wonder What Bin.

Imagine That

Imagine God's people getting settled in Babylon for 70 years. Build houses, gardens, and other buildings to help them settle and feel hopeful each day.

Ask: If you were building a house for you and your family, what would you want it to be like?

Say: Even though they hoped for new houses in Judah someday, God's people settled into life in Babylon. God gave them hope for that day and in the future. God gives us hope. *(It's true!)*

Let's Play

Choose someone to stand in the middle of the group. Pass the ball to others, trying to keep it away from that person. When the middle person gets the ball, the person who threw it must replace him or her in the middle.

Ask: How did you feel when you were trying to get the ball?

Say: Sometimes being the person in the middle felt hopeless! Would things ever change? In hard times, let's remember that God won't leave us, God loves us, and God gives us hope. *(It's true!)*

As kids play, meander around the area, using these questions and comments to connect each activity to today's Bible verse and Bible Point.

Create

Make a memory game! Find two matching stickers and place them on two different index cards. Make several pairs of cards, then combine all the cards and turn them facedown. Take turns flipping over two cards to find a match.

Ask: What helped you remember where certain stickers were located in this game?

Say: We can find hope every day as we look for God and all the good things he has given us—including friends like you!

Lesson 6

Review Together (5 minutes)

Explore a Jesus Connection and work together to create actions for words in the Bible verse.

Supplies:
- Here & Home papers (1 per child)
- crayons

Say: Even when things don't go as we want them to, <u>God gives us hope</u>. *(It's true!)* **Through Jesus, we have the best hope ever—that someday God will make everything right and good and we'll live forever in heaven with God and his children. What a day that will be!**

Let's create some actions to do as we say Jeremiah 29:11 all together. Rather than *me* telling you what to do, you kids can create the actions for us. You're in charge!

Invite kids to work together to make up actions for these words:
- For I know
- the plans I have for you
- says the Lord
- good and not disaster
- future and a hope

Say Jeremiah 29:11 together with actions:

" 'For I know the plans I have for you,' says the Lord. 'They are plans for good and not for disaster, to give you a future and a hope.' "

When we're friends with God, the future is bright. We'll go through some dark days and tough times, but we can look forward to good things ahead because <u>God gives us hope</u>. *(It's true!)*

Take some time to affirm kids by name, mentioning something specific you hope for them this week.

Here & Home

Give kids each the Here & Home paper on page 79. Invite them to color and complete the Bible verse page now, and point out the activity for them to lead their parents in at home.

God Gives Us Hope

Here

Color this image according to the color key. But before you begin, change the plan and choose a different color for each number. Then color according to your new key. Even when plans change, God gives us hope!

> " 'For I know the plans I have for you,' says the Lord. 'They are plans for good and not for disaster, to give you a future and a hope.' "
> Jeremiah 29:11

Color Key
1 = Blue   2 = Purple   3 = Red   4 = Yellow   5 = Orange   6 = Green

Permission to copy this resource from All Together Sunday School granted for local church use.
Copyright © 2024 Group Publishing, Inc., Loveland, CO. group.com

Home

God Gives Us Hope

" 'For I know the plans I have for you,' says the Lord. 'They are plans for good and not for disaster, to give you a future and a hope' " (Jeremiah 29:11).

God inspired people to write the words in the Bible for people to hear or read. Throughout history, people have read the Bible in order to know God and his story better. And yet it's helpful to remember that the original inspired writers did not write *to* people today.

Jeremiah did not address his letter "Dear 21st Century Christian." Rather, he wrote to a specific group of people—the Judean exiles living in Babylon after the fall of Jerusalem.

The words of Jeremiah 29:11 speak to people living in hopeless exile. Families whose plans had been altered by tragedy. A community whose hopes had been smashed with Jerusalem's walls.

Yet, as we read these words from God today, it's okay for you to acknowledge your family's mangled plans and hopeless longings. The God who had hope and a future for the exiles in Babylon still offers hope and a future for his children today—including the people in your family.

May hope comfort your hearts and remind you to trust that God has good things in store for your family—today and for eternity.

Fun Fact

The last king of Judah was Zedekiah. He was 21 years old when he became king. He was stubborn and refused to turn back to God, and, well...things didn't turn out so well for him. Read all about it in 2 Kings 24:18–25:7. Parents of young children, be ready to paraphrase the last part!

Think & Talk

What's one good thing you hope will happen today? What will still be true if that hope doesn't come true?

Read & Do

Read Jeremiah 29:11-14. These words were part of Jeremiah's letter to the exiles in Babylon. Together, write a letter or card to encourage someone who is going through a hard time. Remind them that God gives us hope.

Say & Pray

Before you start up the car engine and head off to a new place, pray and thank God for going with you. Tell God you're looking forward to the good things that will happen today.

Lesson 6

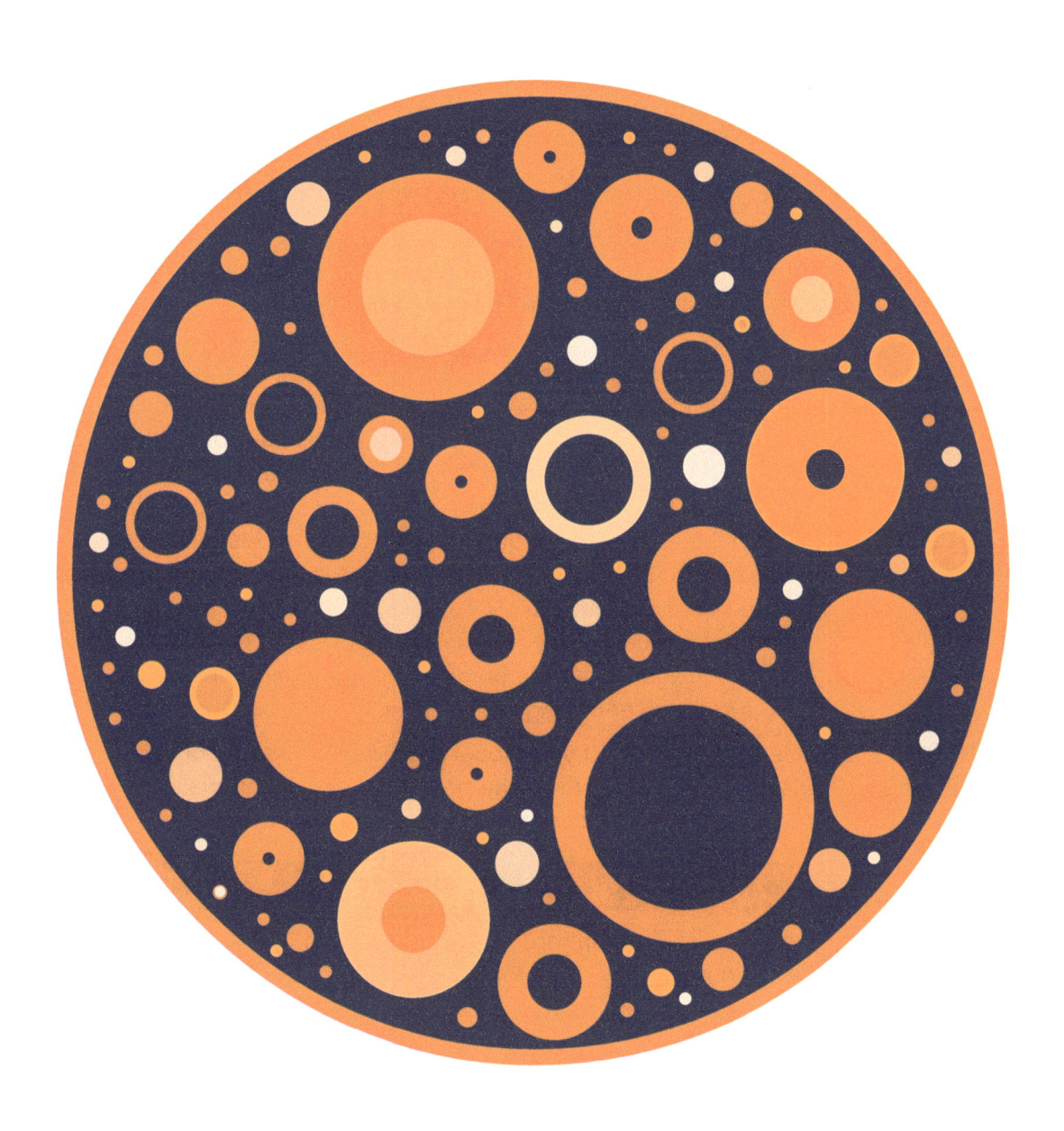

Lesson 7

Jesus Cares

"Then Jesus said, 'Come to me, all of you who are weary and carry heavy burdens, and I will give you rest' " (Matthew 11:28).

Discover Matthew 11:28

When we feel tired, it's good to get some sleep. But what do we do when we're tired *of something*? Tired of trying and failing. Tired of coping with broken friendships, broken promises, and a world broken by sin. Tired of working hard to prove yourself. To whom do we go with that kind of weariness?

In *The Message*, Eugene Peterson paraphrases Jesus' words in Matthew 11:28-30. He writes: "Are you tired? Worn out? Burned out on religion? Come to me. Get away with me and you'll recover your life. I'll show you how to take a real rest. Walk with me and work with me—watch how I do it. Learn the unforced rhythms of grace. I won't lay anything heavy or ill-fitting on you. Keep company with me and you'll learn to live freely and lightly."

That sounds refreshing, doesn't it? We can rest easy because Jesus cares! He hasn't left us to fend for ourselves. Because of Jesus, we don't have to work so hard to be close friends with God. Jesus has done the work, and we get to receive rest from him.

- As you wearily prep lesson supplies, Jesus cares.
- When you feel a little burned out on teaching, Jesus cares.
- If kids' never-ending energy wears you out, Jesus cares.

Jesus cares. About you. About the kids you lead. About your need for a savior. You don't need to be the perfect leader. Simply walk with Jesus through these experiences and watch him work in kids' hearts and lives.

PRAYER

Dear Jesus, I'm coming. I'll rest in you. I'm trusting you to work through me today. Thanks for caring about me and for me. Amen.

Not-So-Fun Fact

Those who first heard Jesus say these words knew that a yoke wasn't something most people wanted to wear at all. In Bible times, a yoke was an instrument made from bent wood that was placed around the necks not only of animals but also of servants. When we read about yokes in the Bible, they symbolize burdens. Jesus lightens the burden of sin in our lives.

Lesson Overview

Bible Verse: Matthew 11:28 | **Bible Point:** Jesus cares. *(It's true!)* | **Bible Exploration:** Matthew 8:14-15; 9:2-7; 11:28-29

Lesson-at-a-Glance

Play Together (10-15 minutes)
Assemble puzzles without looking at the picture on the box and/or complete exercise challenges.

Talk Together | Pray Together (10 minutes)
Talk about how you're feeling today, then pray and talk with God about it.

Bible Discovery (10-15 minutes)
Find and read Matthew 11:28 together, try to draw a perfect circle with and without help, then rest and talk with Jesus.

Wonder What Stations (15-20 minutes)
Choose and move through the following activities:
- Take a Look: Rest and look through children's Bibles and picture books.
- Let's Play: Guide a battery-operated remote control car along a road and think about how Jesus guides our lives.
- Imagine That: Use cookie cutters to shape play dough.

Review Together (5 minutes)
Work together to create actions for words in the Bible verse, and give out Here & Home papers.

Supply List

- ☐ Bible bookmarked at Matthew 11:28
- ☐ All Together Tasks labels (1 sheet for every 8 kids) (on page 8)
- ☐ Feelings Charts (1 for every 2 kids) (on page 9)
- ☐ smartphone timer
- ☐ paper
- ☐ crayons
- ☐ cups (1 per person)
- ☐ Here & Home papers (1 per child) (on page 91)

Wonder What Bin Contents

- ☐ boxed puzzles
- ☐ children's Bibles and picture books
- ☐ pillows and blankets
- ☐ battery-operated remote control car or toy (or kid-powered vehicle will work, too)
- ☐ painter's tape
- ☐ play dough
- ☐ cookie cutters

The "Wonder What Bin"

This supply box is a key part of each All Together Sunday School lesson. This large container will store all the toys and supplies needed for the Play Together activities and Wonder What Stations. Each week, kids will "wonder what" is in store for them! Your Wonder What Bin could be a plastic storage bin, a treasure chest, a toy box, or any large container.

Lesson 7

All Together Tasks

Supplies: All Together Tasks labels (1 sheet for every 8 kids)

As kids arrive, explain the special jobs and encourage each child to choose one to do today. Download and print the All Together Tasks labels or copy them from page 8, and let kids choose the jobs they want to do. It's okay if more than one child has the same job or if one child has a few jobs. Teachers can have another job, too!

Kids choose from the following jobs:

Ready Reader is ready and willing to read a Bible verse aloud.

Prayer Person prays aloud nice and loud so everyone can hear.

Happy Helpers jump at the chance to hand out supplies and clean up stuff.

Befrienders are on the lookout for those who need help and support.

Greeters say, "Hello and welcome!" to everyone as they arrive and "Have a good day!" to everyone as they leave.

Play Together (10-15 minutes)

Play with the kids, using their favorite toys and games to help introduce the Bible Point. Choose one or both activities.

Supplies:
- Wonder What Bin

Puzzled

Work together to assemble a puzzle—without looking at the picture on the box. Dump out the pieces and try to put them together without a guide. Then, after trying for a bit, have someone reveal the picture and hold it while you work together to complete the puzzle.

Ask: What was it like trying to put together a puzzle without a picture to guide you?

Say: Perhaps you were tired of trying and failing to find pieces that go together. You may have grown weary of this activity and been ready to stop. But when you had the guide, it wasn't so hard anymore—in fact, it was fun! Today we'll explore words that Jesus said to people who were weary. Jesus' words show us that Jesus cares.

Rest-er-size

Set a smartphone timer for 60 seconds, and place it where kids can see. Challenge kids to run in place for 60 seconds, then do jumping jacks for 30 seconds, then spin in circles for 10 seconds. Welcome kids to collapse and rest in their seats or on the floor when the challenges are complete.

Ask: How do you feel after all that movement and work? What things in your life make you feel tired and weary—like you just need a rest?

Say: We may get tired when we're playing at recess, doing math problems, or just having to stand in line for a long time. Life makes people tired! It's good to know that Jesus cares when we're tired. Today we'll explore how friendship with Jesus gives us much-needed rest.

Talk Together (5 minutes)

> Kids talk in pairs about how they're feeling today.

Say: Today we'll talk with God and hear what God has to say to us through words in the Bible. But first, let's talk together. How are you feeling today?

Form pairs, and give each pair a Feelings Chart and a crayon. Have partners each circle the face that reflects how they're feeling in this moment and then tell their partners why they chose that face. Be sure to find a partner, too, and participate with the kids as they chat.

Pray Together (5 minutes)

> Kids tell God how they're feeling and pray a prayer all together.

Say: Thanks for talking with a friend! Like we just talked with our friends, we can talk with God! Sometimes we start our prayers with "Dear God," and other times we might say "Dear Jesus." We may even start our prayer with "Holy Spirit." When we pray, God the Father, God the Son, and God the Holy Spirit all hear us and care about what we have to say.

Invite kids to get comfortable and close their eyes as they pray. **Since we're hearing a Bible story about Jesus today, let's address our prayer to him.**

Pray: Dear Jesus, we want to tell you how we feel today and why we feel that way. Pause for several moments of silent prayer. **Thanks for listening, Jesus.**

Say: Now let's pray all together. We'll ask Jesus to guide our time together today.

Watch and do what I do! After each sentence, I'll pause and we'll say the words "All together" together!

Pray: Dear Jesus,

> **May we love** [make the shape of a heart with your hands]
> **you and each other.** ("All together!")
>
> **May we listen** [cup hand behind ear]
> **to you and each other.** ("All together!")
>
> **May we learn** [point to brain]
> **about you and each other.** ("All together!")
>
> **May we laugh and have fun** [high-five a friend]
> **with you and each other.** ("All together!")
>
> **Thanks for bringing us** ("All together!") **today. Amen.**

Supplies:
- Feelings Charts (1 for every 2 kids)
- crayons

Download and print or make one copy of the Feelings Chart on page 9 for every two people. Instead of printing each week, consider placing the charts in plastic sheet protectors. Then kids can use dry-erase markers to mark how they're feeling. Simply clean off the markings for next week!

This prayer will set the tone for your time together each day. Each sentence helps to communicate the values in your classroom and invites God to help everyone do their part, no matter their age! When behavior challenges arise, you can guide kids back to this prayer to steer them toward loving behaviors.

Lesson 7   85

📖 Bible Discovery (15 minutes)

Find and read a verse together, explore its Bible context, and talk about stories in the Bible that reinforce the main idea of the verse.

Supplies:
- Bible bookmarked at Matthew 11:28
- paper
- crayons
- cups (1 per person)
- Wonder What Bin

Find and read Matthew 11:28.

Say: Let's hear a Bible verse that'll help us get to know Jesus even better. Today we'll explore Matthew 11:28.

The Bible is one book, but it's made up of separate *books, chapters,* and *verses*. Chapters are longer and verses are shorter—usually about one sentence.

Let's hear Matthew 11:28. Matthew is the book, "11" is the chapter, and "28" is the verse. These are words that Jesus said to his friends and other people who got to see and hear Jesus when he lived on earth.

Invite the Ready Reader to read the verse from your marked Bible. Have everyone air high-five the Ready Reader to say "thank you" for reading.

Ask: What does this verse tell us about Jesus?

Say: Jesus cares! When people are tired and feel overwhelmed, Jesus cares. Jesus welcomes people to go to him for help—that includes you and me. Why? Because Jesus cares.

That's our Bible Point today. So every time you hear the words "Jesus cares," give two thumbs up and say, "It's true!" To practice, repeat the Bible Point and response several times.

The word *weary* means "tired."

Ask: What do you do when you're tired of something?

Say: When we're tired of something, we want to stop! We may be tired of doing homework, tired of eating vegetables, or tired of waiting our turn. At nighttime we get tired of being awake!

Let's experience what it's like to get tired of something.

Try to draw a perfect circle.

Give each person a piece of paper and a crayon. **Try as hard as you can to draw a perfect circle. Don't let it become lopsided or look more like an egg. Try *really* hard to make a round and beautiful circle.**

Observe everyone as they draw. When you see imperfections, say something like "Close, but try again" or "I see you're working hard, but it's still not perfect." After some time, ask:

Ask: Who is tired of trying to make a perfect circle? Invite responses and reactions from the group.

Ask: Why are you tired of it?

86   All Together Sunday School Book 1

Say: Jesus was talking to people who had been trying really hard to obey a bunch of rules that told them how to live as God's people. They were working really hard to be good enough for God. And they weren't able to do it. But Jesus cared about their weariness. Jesus wanted them to know that they could come to him for help. He could bring them close to God! They weren't perfect—but he was!

Use a cup to draw a perfect circle.

Let's try drawing circles again. This time let's get some help. Show kids how to place the rim of a plastic cup on the paper and trace around the rim to make a beautiful circle. Then let kids use cups to do the same. Encourage kids to fill their papers with circles.

Ask: How did the cup help you make a circle? How is that like Jesus helping people want to be close to God?

Say: Sin in our world and in our hearts keeps people from being close to God. Sin causes people to make wrong choices. God is perfect, and people are not. But Jesus, God's Son, lived a perfect life on earth. He never sinned! And when Jesus died on the cross and came back to life again, he made a way for all people to be forgiven of sin. Listen to the verse again. I'll read the verse that comes after it, too.

Read Matthew 11:28-29 again.

<u>Jesus cares</u>. *(It's true!)* He cares that we need help. When we trust Jesus, we can stop trying to be perfect and let Jesus help us live as God's dearly loved children.

Draw faces in circles to show how people felt about Jesus.

Ask: How do you feel knowing that Jesus cares about you and wants to help you?

Say: Draw a face that shows how you feel in one of your circles. Allow time, then invite kids to share what faces they drew and why they feel that way.

A lot of people went to Jesus for help when he lived on earth. Some may have felt sad because they were sick. Invite everyone to draw a sad face in a circle. **When people were sad because they were sick, Jesus made them healthy again, like Peter's mother-in-law. Listen to this!**

Read aloud Matthew 8:14-15.

Some people who went to Jesus felt tired because their bodies didn't work well. Have everyone draw a tired face in another circle. **And Jesus healed their bodies!**

Lesson 7 87

Read aloud Matthew 9:2-7.

Jesus healed that man and forgave his sins. But the teachers of religious law weren't happy about that. Have everyone draw a mad face in another circle. **They were the ones working so hard to be perfect and obey all the rules. They wouldn't go to Jesus to find rest and help. They kept trying to be good enough for God on their own.**

It's sad, but not everyone goes to Jesus. Not everyone believes that Jesus cares. Not everyone welcomes the gift of rest from Jesus. Still, <u>Jesus cares</u>. *(It's true!)* **When people go to Jesus, he's ready to help them rest in his love and his forgiveness.**

Pray together.

When we rest, we feel comfortable. We can relax and stop doing hard stuff. Let's move to a more comfortable spot now. Grab a pillow or blanket, and choose a spot in our room where you can rest and talk with Jesus.

Allow time for kids to choose pillows and blankets from the Wonder What Bin and then find a comfy spot to rest and pray.

Now that we're cozy, let's think a prayer to Jesus. Think about what's making you tired today—Jesus knows what you're thinking! Or just sit quietly and think about how much Jesus loves and cares for you. We'll rest with Jesus for about two minutes. Prayer Person, I'll let you know when it's time to pray out loud so we can all talk with Jesus together to end our rest time.

After two minutes, signal for the Prayer Person to pray a simple prayer or simply say "Amen!"

Wonder What Stations (15-20 minutes)

> Kids will wonder and wander their way through these three free-flowing application activities. Young kids may gravitate toward some things while older kids are drawn to others.

Say: **Let's keep exploring Matthew 11:28 with the items in this Wonder What Bin. You'll have three choices—I wonder what you'll choose to do first!**

Supplies:
- Wonder What Bin

Dramatically re-reveal what's inside the Wonder What Bin, and explain these three different options for kids to choose during a free-play time. After 15-20 minutes, tell kids you'll be cleaning up the Wonder What Stations in about a minute. Have Happy Helpers return supplies to the Wonder What Bin.

Take a Look

You can keep resting with Jesus! Read some books, look through some Bible stories, or just take some time to think or chat quietly with a friend.

Ask: **What other activities are restful for you?**

Say: **Jesus is with us as we rest and relax. Jesus cares!** *(It's true!)* **He gives us activities to help us rest with him.**

Let's Play

Use painter's tape to make a road for the car. Additionally, make a garage where it can "rest." Use the controller to guide the car along the road and into the garage, then let someone else take it for a spin.

Ask: **What about guiding the car reminds you of how Jesus guides our lives?**

Say: **On our own, we may not know where to go or what to do. And eventually we'll run out of charge! But when we invite Jesus to control our lives, he guides us and gives us all we need.**

As kids play, meander around the area, using these questions and comments to connect each activity to today's Bible verse and Bible Point.

Imagine That

Use cookie cutters to help you shape play dough into different things, like cookies, people, or animals.

Ask: **How do the cookie cutters help you create things?**

Say: **When you use cookie cutters, you don't have to work so hard to shape play dough into cool things. Since Jesus cares** *(It's true!)*, **we trust that Jesus will guide and shape us into close friends with God.**

Review Together (5 minutes)

> Work together to create actions for words in the Bible verse.

Supplies:
- Here & Home papers (1 per child)
- crayons

Say: <u>Jesus cares</u>. *(It's true!)* **When we trust Jesus, we can stop working hard to be perfect and let Jesus help us live as God's dearly loved children.**

Let's create some actions to do as we say Matthew 11:28 all together. Rather than *me* telling you what to do, you kids can create the actions for us. You're in charge!

Invite kids to work together to make up actions for these words:

- Come to me
- all of you who are weary
- carry heavy burdens
- give you rest

Say Matthew 11:28 together with actions:

"Then Jesus said, 'Come to me, all of you who are weary and carry heavy burdens, and I will give you rest.'"

<u>Jesus cares</u>. *(It's true!)* **No matter what your day is like or what you are going through, Jesus invites you to go to him and find rest.**

Take some time to affirm kids by name, reminding each person that Jesus cares for him or her.

Here & Home

Give kids each the Here & Home paper on page 91. Invite them to color and complete the Bible verse page now, and point out the activity for them to lead their parents in at home.

Jesus Cares Here

Color this picture as you rest with Jesus. What things on this page help you rest?

"Then Jesus said, 'Come to me, all of you who are weary and carry heavy burdens, and I will give you rest.'"

Matthew 11:28

Permission to copy this resource from All Together Sunday School granted for local church use.
Copyright © 2024 Group Publishing, Inc., Loveland, CO. group.com

Here & Home Lesson 7

Home

Jesus Cares

"Then Jesus said, 'Come to me, all of you who are weary and carry heavy burdens, and I will give you rest' " (Matthew 11:28).

When we're tired, it's good to get some sleep. But what do we do when we're tired *of something*? Tired of trying hard. Tired of people not getting along. Tired of trying to not mess up. Who can we go to with that kind of weariness?

Jesus, that's who.

His words in Matthew 11:28 apply to us, too! "Come to me…and I will give you rest."

Ahh! That sounds rather refreshing, doesn't it? We don't have to be perfect on our own. We don't have to get through tough stuff on our own. We don't have to try to be good enough for God on our own. Jesus cares. And he's made a way for us to be close friends with God—forever!

Not-So-Fun Fact

People in Bible times knew that a yoke wasn't something most people wanted to wear at all. In Bible times, a yoke was an instrument made from bent wood that was placed around the necks of animals and servants. When we read about yokes in the Bible, they symbolize burdens or heavy stuff.

Read & Do

Find a comfy, cozy spot for a rest. Then read Matthew 11:28 aloud. After you've read the verse, stay comfy with Jesus until you're ready to get moving again!

Think & Talk

What was your favorite part of today?

Say & Pray

Think about Jesus when you're tucked in bed, ready for some rest. Whisper to him all the ways he's cared for you today. Then say, "Thank you!"

Lesson 7

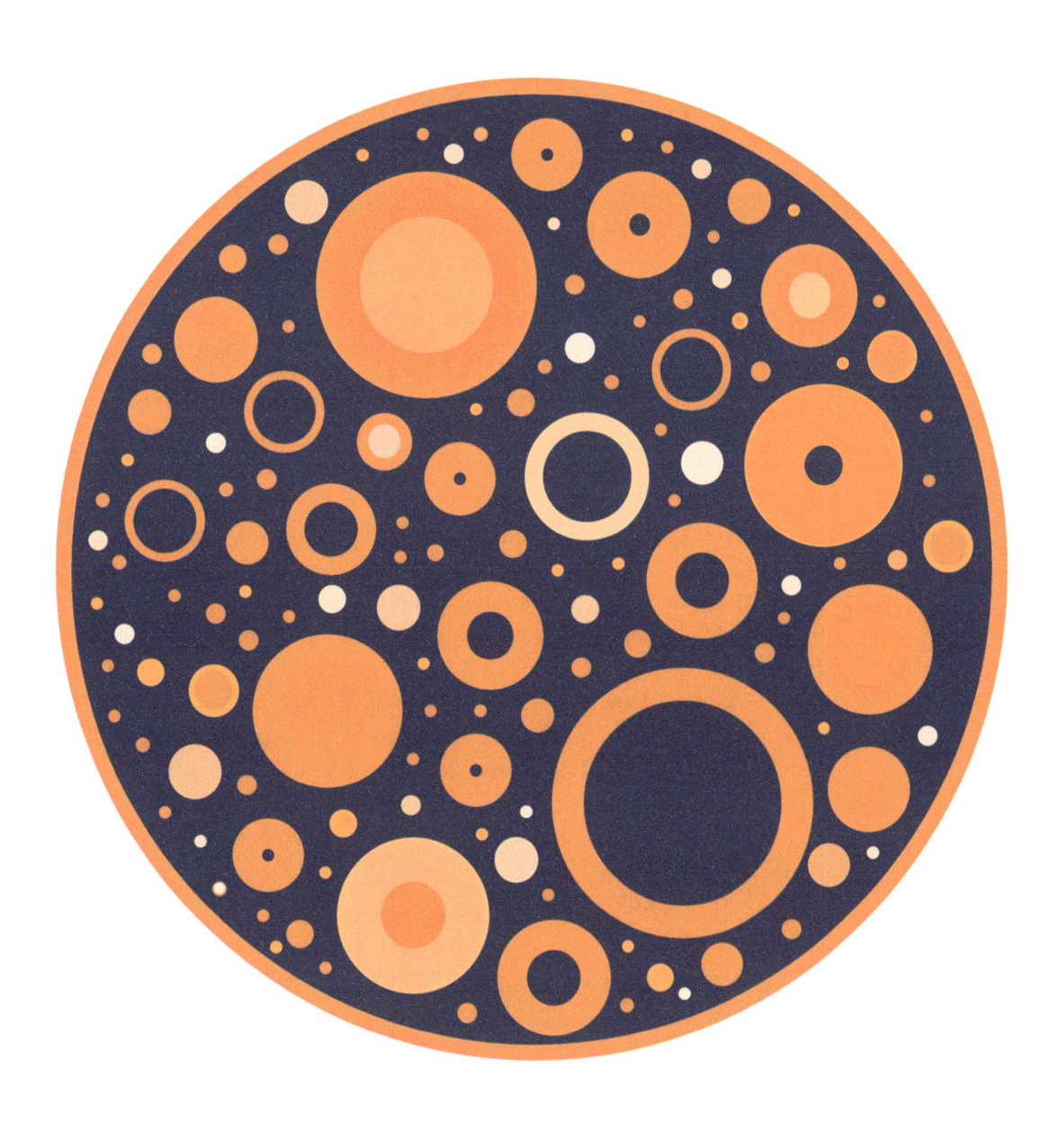

Lesson 8: Jesus Loves Children

"Let the children come to me. Don't stop them! For the Kingdom of God belongs to those who are like these children" (Mark 10:14).

Discover Mark 10:14

Consider the places you've gone this week. Which locations would you judge "kid friendly"? Some restaurants may be a little fancy. Many workplaces are rather stuffy. Movies theaters are full of PG-13 movies. And kids may not be ready to accompany parents to the gym, either.

Jesus' disciples would add wherever Jesus was to that list. They assumed that proximity to Jesus was a kid-free zone. And boy were they wrong!

Mark 10:14 reveals that Jesus cared about children. Jesus loves children, and he pointed to kids as examples of what God wants from his grown-up children, too. As God's children, we're allowed—in fact welcomed—to have a pure and simple dependency on God. We don't have to muddle through life on our own.

So as you lead this lesson, depend on God. Like a child depends on a caregiver to provide nourishment, direction, and safety, rely on God to lead and guide your time with his kids today.

Jesus loves children. How will kids experience that love through you today?

- Model Jesus' love as you play together.
- Show Jesus' love as you attentively listen to what they have to say.
- Display Jesus' love, even during not-so-lovable moments.

And that's not all! Don't forget to watch for ways *children* show *you* what Jesus' love is like, too. "For the Kingdom of God belongs to those who are like these children." Enjoy your front-row-seat view of this truth as you lead this lesson.

PRAYER

Dear Jesus, thank you for loving the children in my life and in this class. Love through me as I lead them. And may I follow their lead and depend on you more and more. Amen.

Fun Fact

The Greek word for *children* used in Mark 10 is *paidia*. That word refers to children ranging from babies to preteens. Jesus welcomed kids of all ages, too!

Lesson Overview

📖 **Bible Verse:** Mark 10:14 | **Bible Point:** Jesus loves children. *(It's true!)* | **Bible Exploration:** Mark 10:13-16

Lesson-at-a-Glance

Play Together (10-15 minutes)
Make a three-legged race and discover what it's like to depend on someone and/or play Wonder What Bin Basketball and try to keep a ball out of the bin.

Talk Together | Pray Together (10 minutes)
Talk about how they're feeling today, then pray and talk with God about it.

Bible Discovery (10-15 minutes)
Find and read Mark 10:14 together, imagine meeting a celebrity, and celebrate cool things about kids.

Wonder What Stations (15-20 minutes)
Choose and move through the following activities:
- Create: Make and receive a gold star—just for being a kid.
- Let's Play: Make an obstacle course.
- Imagine That: Shape chenille wires into a self-portrait, then play with the mini-me!

Review Together (5 minutes)
Work together to create actions for words in the Bible verse, and give out Here & Home papers.

Supply List

- ☐ Bible bookmarked at Mark 10:13-16
- ☐ All Together Tasks labels (1 sheet for every 8 kids) (on page 8)
- ☐ Feelings Charts (1 for every 2 kids) (on page 9)
- ☐ Here & Home papers (1 per child) (on page 103)
- ☐ crayons

Wonder What Bin Contents

- ☐ stretchy elastic headbands
- ☐ playground ball
- ☐ chenille wires
- ☐ hula hoops
- ☐ foam stars
- ☐ double-sided tape
- ☐ craft supplies such as glitter glue, markers, and stickers

The "Wonder What Bin"

This supply box is a key part of each All Together Sunday School lesson. This large container will store all the toys and supplies needed for the Play Together activities and Wonder What Stations. Each week, kids will "wonder what" is in store for them! Your Wonder What Bin could be a plastic storage bin, a treasure chest, a toy box, or any large container.

Lesson 8   95

All Together Tasks

Supplies: All Together Tasks labels (1 sheet for every 8 kids)

As kids arrive, explain the special jobs and encourage each child to choose one to do today. Download and print the All Together Tasks labels or copy them from page 8, and let kids choose the jobs they want to do. It's okay if more than one child has the same job or if one child has a few jobs. Teachers can have another job, too!

Kids choose from the following jobs:

Ready Reader is ready and willing to read a Bible verse aloud.

Prayer Person prays aloud nice and loud so everyone can hear.

Happy Helpers jump at the chance to hand out supplies and clean up stuff.

Befrienders are on the lookout for those who need help and support.

Greeters say, "Hello and welcome!" to everyone as they arrive and "Have a good day!" to everyone as they leave.

Play Together (10-15 minutes)

Play with the kids, using their favorite toys and games to help introduce the Bible Point. Choose one or both activities.

Supplies:
- Wonder What Bin

Three-Legged Race

Make a three-legged race! Pair up, stand beside each other, and use a stretchy elastic headband to connect your ankles together. (Or tie shoelaces together!) Decide on a spot across the room, and work together to move to that spot. Count to see how long it takes for pairs to get across the room, then see if they can improve their time coming back.

Say: When we depend on someone, we rely on that person. We need that person to help us get where we need to go and do what we need to do.

Ask: As a kid, who do you depend on?

Say: Today we'll discover that dependence is a good thing! Jesus loves children because depending on people comes naturally to kids like you.

Wonder What Bin Basketball

Play basketball with the Wonder What Bin and a playground ball! Choose one or two people to "defend" the bin while others dribble the playground ball around the bin before trying to toss the ball into the bin and score. Rotate so there are new defenders after each "basket."

Ask: When you play a sport, do you like to play offense, where you score points, or defense, where you try to keep people from scoring? Tell why.

Say: Good game, everyone. You tried to keep the ball out of the bin. Well, in today's Bible story, people tried to keep children away from Jesus. It didn't work so well because Jesus loves children. Nothing and no one can keep you from a close friendship with Jesus.

Talk Together (5 minutes)

> Kids talk in pairs about how they're feeling today.

Say: Today we'll talk with God and hear what God has to say to us through words in the Bible. But first, let's talk together. How are you feeling today?

Form pairs, and give each pair a Feelings Chart and a crayon. Have partners each circle the face that reflects how they're feeling in this moment and then tell their partners why they chose that face. Be sure to find a partner, too, and participate with the kids as they chat.

Supplies:
- Feelings Charts (1 for every 2 kids)
- crayons

Download and print or make one copy of the Feelings Chart on page 9 for every two people. Instead of printing each week, consider placing the charts in plastic sheet protectors. Then kids can use dry-erase markers to mark how they're feeling. Simply clean off the markings for next week!

Pray Together (5 minutes)

> Kids tell God how they're feeling and pray a prayer all together.

Say: Thanks for talking with a friend! In the Bible, we read that we can pray and tell God anything. You'll see the words of that Bible verse printed on the Feelings Chart. If you'd like to read along, please do!

Philippians 4:6 says, "Pray about everything. Tell God what you need, and thank him for all he has done."

Like we just talked with our friends, we can talk with God! Let's practice doing that now! We'll think a prayer and tell God how we're feeling today. After our thinking prayer, we'll pray a special prayer all together.

Invite kids to get comfortable and close their eyes as they pray.

Pray: Dear God, we want to think with you and tell you how we feel today and why we feel that way. *Pause for several moments of silent prayer.* **Thanks for listening, God.**

Say: Now let's pray all together. We'll ask God to guide our time together today.

Watch and do what I do! After each sentence, I'll pause and we'll say the words "All together" together!

Pray: Dear God,

May we love [make the shape of a heart with your hands] **you and each other.** ("All together!")

May we listen [cup hand behind ear] **to you and each other.** ("All together!")

May we learn [point to brain] **about you and each other.** ("All together!")

May we laugh and have fun [high-five a friend] **with you and each other.** ("All together!")

Thanks for bringing us ("All together!") **today. Amen.**

This prayer will set the tone for your time together each day. Each sentence helps to communicate the values in your classroom and invites God to help everyone do their part, no matter their age! When behavior challenges arise, you can guide kids back to this prayer to steer them toward loving behaviors.

📖 Bible Discovery (15 minutes)

Find and read a verse together, explore its Bible context, and talk about stories in the Bible that reinforce the main idea of the verse.

Supplies:
- Bible bookmarked at Mark 10:14
- Wonder What Bin

Find and read Mark 10:14.

Say: Let's hear a Bible verse that'll help us get to know Jesus better. Today we'll explore Mark 10:14.

The Bible has different books, but it's also divided into two parts. The Old Testament is the first part, and the New Testament is the second part. Mark is the second book of the New Testament. Mark tells true stories about Jesus!

Listen to Mark 10:14.

Invite the Ready Reader to read the verse from your marked Bible. Have everyone clap to thank the Ready Reader for reading.

Ask: What does this verse tell us about Jesus?

Say: This verse leads me to believe that Jesus likes kids! In fact, <u>Jesus loves children</u>. That's our Bible Point today. So every time you hear the words "Jesus loves children," give two thumbs up and say, "It's true!" To practice, repeat the Bible Point and response several times.

Let's find out what happened before Jesus said those words. It was something that made Jesus really mad!

Ask: What things make you mad?

Say: You might get mad when toys break, when people do or say something you don't like, or when someone is picking on someone you love. Well, it turns out some people were picking on other people Jesus loved. And he didn't like it one bit. Listen to what happened.

📖 Read aloud Mark 10:13.

Imagine meeting a celebrity!

Let's imagine you're the kids in the story, and Jesus is sitting on the Wonder What Bin. Let's head over to Jesus! Move with everyone and have a seat on the floor.

Here we are! You see, Jesus was like a celebrity. All sorts of people wanted to meet Jesus, be near him, and maybe even shake his hand and touch him! Invite kids to shake hands with a neighbor and say, "Nice to meet you!"

Ask: A celebrity is a famous person. What famous person would you want to meet? Share a kid-friendly example from your life to begin. Perhaps a sports star, a musician, or an actor.

Say: Think of the people we just mentioned. Name a few again.

Ask: How would you feel if your parents took you to meet those people? Let's use our Feelings Chart again to show how you'd feel.

Invite kids to pick an emoji from the chart to show how'd they feel to meet a celebrity.

Say: We'd feel all sorts of emotions! Our hearts might feel happy. Have kids make hearts with their hands, hold them up to their faces, and smile inside the hearts. **Our knees might bounce with excitement.** Have kids stand and bounce up and down. **And there may be a few nervous butterflies in our stomachs, too!** Have kids flap and move like butterflies for a few moments, then ask the "butterflies" to come in for a landing.

We'd have those feelings meeting a great big celebrity today. And the children who got to meet Jesus might have felt the same way! Their parents brought them to Jesus—but listen to what made Jesus mad.

📖 Read aloud Mark 10:13-14.

The kids didn't make Jesus mad—his grown-up friends did! The disciples were Jesus' friends. They spend a lot of time with Jesus. So much time that maybe they started to think they were pretty big stuff. They were besties with a celebrity, after all! Imagine you're a disciple, sit up tall, and puff your chest out a little—like you're big stuff. Allow time.

But Jesus didn't think they were big stuff. <u>Jesus loves children</u>. *(It's true!)* **He** *wanted* **the kids to come to him, and he** *didn't want* **his friends to stop them. Listen to the rest of the story.**

📖 Read aloud Mark 10:15-16.

Group hug! Gather kids together for a hug or a huddle. Once you're all together, shout, "Jesus loves children!" and invite kids to shout, "It's true!" Repeat several times, encouraging kids to get louder and louder. Then return to your original seats.

Celebrate kids!

Earlier, Jesus heard the disciples talking about who was the greatest. So he put a little child among them and said that anyone who welcomed a child welcomed him and his Father, God (Mark 9:36-37). **<u>Jesus really loves children</u>!** *(It's true!)*

Some people who study the Bible think Jesus loved and welcomed children because kids are really good at showing grown-ups how to depend on God. That's because you kids are good at depending on *people***.**

Ask: Who have you depended on today? What did that person do for you?

Say: Kids like you are good at depending on God, too. Tell a story about a time the kids you teach, or some kids you know, encouraged your faith in God.

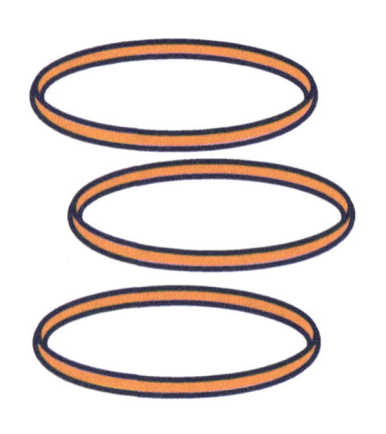

Your dependence on God makes you pretty great. You show grown-ups what true greatness looks like. I'm glad I get to see that greatness during our time today!

Here's something cool. We can't see Jesus in a man's body sitting on that Wonder What Bin over there, but Jesus is still here with us in this room. Through the power of the Holy Spirit, Jesus is always with us. So even though it may feel a little silly. Let's all say "hi" to Jesus. Allow time. **If you want to, you can tell Jesus that you love him, too!** Allow time.

Jesus is with us, and he's happy to see each one of you today. So let's roll out the red carpet and celebrate each kid here! Look inside the Wonder What Bin. **Well, I don't have a red carpet today. But I do have hula hoops!**

Place the hula hoops on the floor in a line, creating a path for kids to walk down. Have everyone gather on either side of the path. Call each kid by name, saying: **Jesus loves** [child's name]. Invite that child to walk, jump, skip, or groove down the path as everyone claps and celebrates that kid. At the end, take a turn yourself—you're one of God's big kids!

Pray together.

<u>Jesus loves children</u>. *(It's true!)* **Just as you are. Just as you'll be. When you're friends with Jesus, he'll love you at each age and stage of your life. You can always depend on him. Let's huddle one more time and pray a thank-you prayer.** Have kids all try to step inside one or two hula hoops. Then lead this prayer.

Pray: Jesus, you love these kids. Their laughter, their loudness, their energy, their questions—everything about them. May they know and feel your love today.

Ask the Prayer Person to pray a simple prayer or simply say "Amen!"

Wonder What Stations (15-20 minutes)

> Kids will wonder and wander their way through these three free-flowing application activities. Young kids may gravitate toward some things while older kids are drawn to others.

Say: Let's keep exploring Mark 10:14 with the items in this Wonder What Bin. You'll have three choices—I wonder what you'll choose to do first!

Dramatically re-reveal what's inside the Wonder What Bin, and explain these three different options for kids to choose during a free-play time. After 15-20 minutes, tell kids you'll be cleaning up the Wonder What Stations in about a minute. Have Happy Helpers return supplies to the Wonder What Bin.

Supplies:
- Wonder What Bin

Create

Kids each get a gold star—just for being a kid! Use markers, stickers, and glitter glue to decorate a foam or paper star. Then add double-sided tape to the back to wear it home!

Ask: How can you shine Jesus' love to other kids this week?

Say: Kids, you don't have to do anything to earn or deserve Jesus' love. Jesus loves children just because you're you! *(It's true!)*

Let's Play

Make an obstacle course using hula hoops, the Wonder What Bin, and other objects in your room. Take turns moving through the course. Time each other to see how fast each person moves through the obstacles. Change up the course whenever you'd like.

Say: Obstacles try to keep us from getting to places we want to go. Who knows what kind of obstacles the disciples wanted to put between kids and Jesus that day! But Jesus loves children. *(It's true!)* **Jesus welcomes kids to come right to him!**

Ask: What can keep people (grown-ups and kids alike) from being close friends with Jesus?

As kids play, meander around the area, using these questions and comments to connect each activity to today's Bible verse and Bible Point.

Imagine That

Use chenille wires to make kids Jesus loves—including you! Cut and twist the wires into a stick figure person, then wrap different colors around to make clothes and hair. Shape wires into hats, purses, or other things you like to carry with you. Then play with the kids, making up stories of things they do throughout their day.

Ask: What's something fun you did this week? What do you think Jesus would say to you about that fun thing?

Say: Jesus loves children. *(It's true!)* **And Jesus loves being part of each moment of your day—and your lives!**

Lesson 8

Review Together (5 minutes)

> Work together to create actions for words in the Bible verse.

Say: When people believe in Jesus and trust that he made a way for them to be forgiven and forever friends with God, they become children of God. That means no matter how old you are, you are still a child of God. You can still depend on God and trust that God's at work, bringing hope and light to our world today—and you can help!

Let's create some actions to do as we say Mark 10:14 all together. Rather than *me* telling you what to do, you kids can create the actions for us. You're in charge! This is a long one, so we'll take one line at a time.

Invite kids to work together to make up actions for these phrases:

- Let the children come
- to me
- Don't stop them!
- Kingdom of God
- belongs to those
- who are like these children

Say Mark 10:14 together with actions:

"Let the children come to me. Don't stop them! For the Kingdom of God belongs to those who are like these children."

Kids, you're pretty great! And I'm so happy to spend time with you today. Thanks for showing me what's important to God. <u>Jesus loves children</u>. *(It's true!)* May you remember and enjoy Jesus' love for you today and every day!

Take some time to affirm kids by name, reminding them of Jesus' love.

Supplies:
- Here & Home papers (1 per child)
- crayons

Here & Home

Give kids each the Here & Home paper on page 103. Invite them to color and complete the Bible verse page now, and point out the activity for them to lead their parents in at home.

Jesus Loves Children

Here

Get to know someone Jesus loves. Form pairs and work together to complete this page for each person.

All About Me

My name:

I am _____ years old.

Draw yourself

Me

"Let the children come to me. Don't stop them! For the Kingdom of God belongs to those who are like these children" (Mark 10:14).

Favorite colors

Favorite show

Big dream

I like...

I don't like...

Favorite book

Permission to copy this resource from All Together Sunday School granted for local church use.
Copyright © 2024 Group Publishing, Inc., Loveland, CO. group.com

Here & Home Lesson 8   103

Home

Jesus Loves Children

"Let the children come to me. Don't stop them! For the Kingdom of God belongs to those who are like these children" (Mark 10:14).

What places in your town aren't very "kid-friendly"? Perhaps certain restaurants, movie theaters, and workplaces aren't places kids readily go.

Jesus' disciples would add wherever Jesus was to that list. They assumed that proximity to Jesus' was a kid-free zone. And boy were they wrong!

Mark 10:14 reveals that Jesus cared about children. Jesus loves children, and he pointed to kids as examples of what God wants from his grown-up children, too. As God's children, we're all allowed—in fact welcomed—to have a pure and simple dependency on God. We don't have to muddle through life on our own. Jesus' love and attention will carry us through!

And, parents, don't forget to watch for ways your children show *you* what Jesus' love is like. "For the Kingdom of God belongs to those who are like these children." Enjoy your front-row-seat view of this truth as you spend time as a family this week.

Fun Fact

The Greek word for *children* used in Mark 10 is *paidia*. (That's the word Jesus would have said aloud!) That word covers an age range of babies to preteens.

Think & Talk

What was your favorite part of today?

Read & Do

Read Mark 10:13-16. Play a game like "Mother May I?" One person stands away from the family and grants permission for family members to move closer in fun ways. Thank Jesus for welcoming kids to be his close friends.

Say & Pray

Then have a family group hug and let the youngest kid pray for each person. Thank Jesus for loving each person.

104 Here & Home Lesson 8

Lesson 8   105

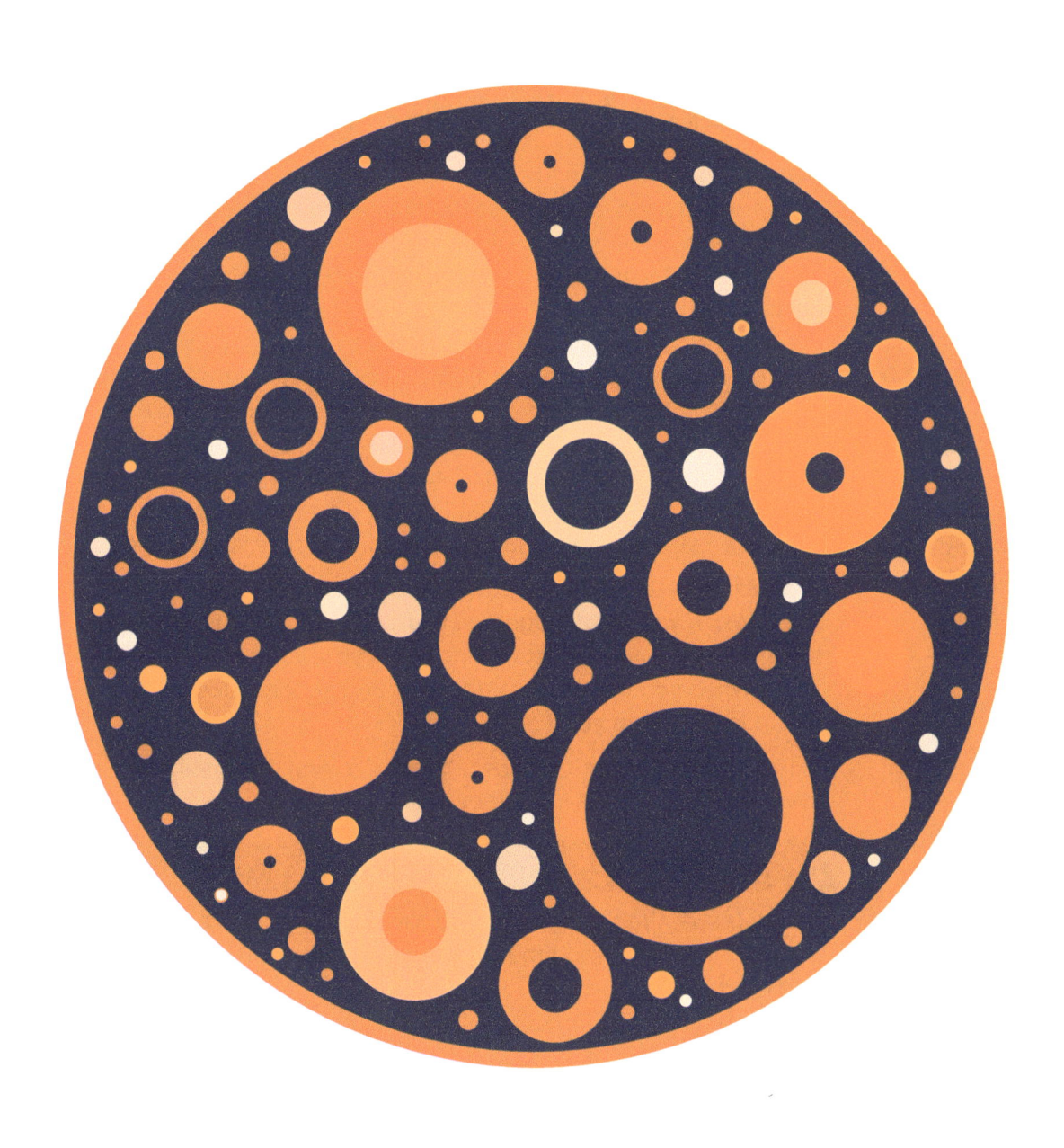

Lesson 9

Jesus Brings Joy

"I bring you good news that will bring great joy to all people. The Savior... has been born" (Luke 2:10-11).

Discover Luke 2:10-11

Have you ever felt like you *should* feel joy? Perhaps it's the Christmas season, and beautiful music, twinkling lights, and happy children are all around. But you feel sad. Or it's springtime! Flowers are blooming, birds are chirping, and your heart is breaking. In those moments, you may not feel joy. But, child of God, you still have it.

Search a dictionary and you'll see that the word *joy* has a variety of definitions, including "a source or cause of delight." For God's children, *Jesus* is the source of great joy. In other words, joy is a delightful gift from Jesus!

In Luke 2:10-11, the angel announced that joy had arrived because Jesus was born. When shepherds were scared, they had joy. When Joseph felt stress, he had joy. When Mary felt tired, she had joy. Why? Because Jesus was there. The Savior of the world had arrived. And he's still with people today.

So as you lead kids today, you have joy.
- When you giggle together, you have joy. Jesus is with you.
- When a game or activity frustrates you, you have joy. Jesus is with you.
- When you feel happy, sad, tired, and all the other things, you have joy. Jesus is with you.

It *is* good news, isn't it? Jesus brings joy. And when you're his friend, you have it. Enjoy that gift all together today.

PRAYER

Dear Jesus, thanks for bringing joy to my life. Your friendship is steady and true, and I'm just so grateful for you. You're my hero. Amen.

Fun Fact

Contrary to cute Christmas pageant costumes, Luke 2 doesn't mention angels' halos or wings. But it was still an out-of-this world experience! Check out the details given as you reread Luke 2:9-14.

Lesson Overview

Bible Verse: Luke 2:10-11 | **Bible Point:** Jesus brings joy. *(It's true!)* | **Bible Exploration:** Luke 2:8-20

Lesson-at-a-Glance

Play Together (10-15 minutes)
Explore what it means to "bring" something. Imagine what you'd bring to a party and/or bring pompoms across the room.

Talk Together | Pray Together (10 minutes)
Talk about how you're feeling today, then pray and talk with God about it.

Bible Discovery (10-15 minutes)
Find and read Luke 2:10-11 together, make a Christmas "Joy Mix" to snack on, and thank Jesus for bringing joy to the world.

Wonder What Stations (15-20 minutes)
Choose and move through the following activities:
- Let's Play: Play pompom Hide-and-Seek.
- Try This: Blow bubbles with straws.
- Take a Look: Look through photos of joy-filled moments.

Review Together (5 minutes)
Work together to create actions for words in the Bible verse, and give out Here & Home papers.

Supply List

- ☐ Bible bookmarked at Luke 2:10-11
- ☐ All Together Tasks labels (1 sheet for every 8 kids) (on page 8)
- ☐ Feelings Charts (1 for every 2 kids) (on page 9)
- ☐ permanent marker
- ☐ serving spoon or tongs
- ☐ cups, napkins, hand cleanser
- ☐ pretzel sticks, mini marshmallows, animal crackers, M&M's candies, Ritz crackers
- ☐ Here & Home papers (1 per child) (on page 115)
- ☐ crayons

Wonder What Bin Contents
- ☐ container of pompoms
- ☐ clear plastic cups
- ☐ dish soap
- ☐ drinking straws
- ☐ water
- ☐ serving tray
- ☐ printed family (or church family) photos of joyful moments

The "Wonder What Bin"

This supply box is a key part of each All Together Sunday School lesson. This large container will store all the toys and supplies needed for the Play Together activities and Wonder What Stations. Each week, kids will "wonder what" is in store for them! Your Wonder What Bin could be a plastic storage bin, a treasure chest, a toy box, or any large container.

Lesson 9

All Together Tasks

Supplies: All Together Tasks labels (1 sheet for every 8 kids)

As kids arrive, explain the special jobs and encourage each child to choose one to do today. Download and print the All Together Tasks labels or copy them from page 8, and let kids choose the jobs they want to do. It's okay if more than one child has the same job or if one child has a few jobs. Teachers can have another job, too!

Kids choose from the following jobs:

Ready Reader is ready and willing to read a Bible verse aloud.

Prayer Person prays aloud nice and loud so everyone can hear.

Happy Helpers jump at the chance to hand out supplies and clean up stuff.

Befrienders are on the lookout for those who need help and support.

Greeters say, "Hello and welcome!" to everyone as they arrive and "Have a good day!" to everyone as they leave.

Play Together (10-15 minutes)

Play with the kids, using their favorite toys and games to help introduce the Bible Point. Choose one or both activities.

Supplies:
- Wonder What Bin

Bring the Pompoms

Put the container of pompoms on one side of your room, then line up across from it. Assign everyone a number. Choose a leader to call a number and a way to move—for example, "Four, hop!" or "Two, gallop!" or "Five, crab walk!" When your number is called, move in that manner to pick up some pompoms and bring them back. Continue until all pompoms have been retrieved.

Say: Your job was to bring pompoms from the other side of the room. When you bring something, you personally deliver it. Today we'll find out that Jesus brings joy. Jesus personally delivered joy to the world!

Ask: When has someone brought something to you? What did that person bring?

Party Planning

Complete this sentence with objects that begin with the letter J. "I'm going to a party, and I'm bringing _____." Give everyone a turn to think of something they'd bring that starts with that letter. Together, come up with at least 10 items. Then let someone choose a new letter and play again.

Say: Those parties sound fun! We bring gifts, food, and even [something listed] to parties. Today we'll find out that Jesus brings joy. Friendship with Jesus brings joy each day of our lives.

Talk Together (5 minutes)

| Kids talk in pairs about how they're feeling today.

Say: Today we'll talk with God and hear what God has to say to us through words in the Bible. But first, let's talk together. How are you feeling today?

Form pairs, and give each pair a Feelings Chart and a crayon. Have partners each circle the face that reflects how they're feeling in this moment and then tell their partners why they chose that face. Be sure to find a partner, too, and participate with the kids as they chat.

Supplies:
- Feelings Charts (1 for every 2 kids)
- crayons

Download and print or make one copy of the Feelings Chart on page 9 for every two people. Instead of printing each week, consider placing the charts in plastic sheet protectors. Then kids can use dry-erase markers to mark how they're feeling. Simply clean off the markings for next week!

Pray Together (5 minutes)

| Kids tell God how they're feeling and pray a prayer all together.

Say: Thanks for sharing with a friend! Today we'll talk about joy. Joy isn't exactly a feeling. It's not on our Feelings Charts. Instead, joy is a gift that Jesus brings. When we're friends with Jesus, we have joy when we feel happy, sad, or any other emotion.

Jesus cares about how we're feeling. Like we just talked with each other, we can talk with Jesus! Let's practice doing that now. We'll silently pray and tell Jesus how we're feeling today. We won't pray with our voices—instead we'll just think a prayer to Jesus for a little bit. After our thinking prayer, we'll pray a special prayer all together.

Invite kids to get comfortable and close their eyes as they pray.

Pray: Dear Jesus, we want to tell you how we feel today and why we feel that way. Pause for several moments of silent prayer. **Thanks for listening, Jesus.**

Say: Now let's pray all together. We'll ask God to guide our time together today.

Watch and do what I do! After each sentence, I'll pause and we'll say the words "All together" together!

Pray: Dear God,

May we love [make the shape of a heart with your hands] **you and each other.** ("All together!")

May we listen [cup hand behind ear] **to you and each other.** ("All together!")

May we learn [point to brain] **about you and each other.** ("All together!")

May we laugh and have fun [high-five a friend] **with you and each other.** ("All together!")

Thanks for bringing us ("All together!") **today. Amen.**

This prayer will set the tone for your time together each day. Each sentence helps to communicate the values in your classroom and invites God to help everyone do their part, no matter their age! When behavior challenges arise, you can guide kids back to this prayer to steer them toward loving behaviors.

Lesson 9

📖 Bible Discovery (15 minutes)

Find and read a verse together, explore its Bible context, and talk about stories in the Bible that reinforce the main idea of the verse.

Supplies:
- Bible bookmarked at Luke 2:10-11
- permanent marker
- serving spoon or tongs
- cups
- napkins
- hand cleanser
- pretzel sticks
- mini marshmallows
- animal crackers
- M&M's candies
- Ritz crackers

*Allergy alert! Ask about food allergies before serving. Consider having alternative, parent-approved snacks available.

Find and read Luke 2:10-11.

Say: Let's hear some verses in the Bible that will help us get to know Jesus even better. Today we'll explore Luke 2:10-11.

Luke 2 is a pretty famous chapter of the Bible because it tells the story of Christmas! If you've ever seen or been part of a Christmas play or pageant, there's a good chance that Luke, chapter 2 was said or read.

Let's hear Luke 2:10-11. An angel said these words to tell about Jesus' birth.

Invite the Ready Reader to read the verse from your marked Bible. Have everyone clap to thank the Ready Reader for reading.

Ask: What does this verse tell us about Jesus?

Say: This verse tells us that Jesus was born and <u>Jesus brings joy</u>! That's our Bible Point today. So every time you hear the words "Jesus brings joy," give two thumbs up and say, "It's true!" To practice, repeat the Bible Point and response several times.

Listen again to what the angel said: "I bring you good news that will bring great joy to all people. The Savior…has been born." That "Savior" is Jesus! A savior is someone who rescues people. A savior is like a hero!

The angel's good news would bring great joy. Well, I have good news that'll bring great joy to you right now—at least I hope it will!

It's snack time! Invite everyone to cheer.

Eat a Christmas story snack.

Today we'll make and eat the Christmas story. How fun is that? We'll make "Joy Mix." It's like trail mix, but each ingredient will remind us about Jesus' birth.

Show kids the ingredients. Invite Happy Helpers and Befrienders to give everyone a cup, a napkin, and some hand sanitizer. Use a permanent marker to write kids' names or initials on their cups in case they want to take some of the snack home.

Joyful snacks need joyful music! Sing a peppy Christmas tune as supplies are distributed and hands are cleansed.

First, we need pretzel sticks. Put a few pretzel sticks in each person's cup. **Pretzel sticks remind me of shepherds who were watching their sheep. The shepherds may have carried staffs that looked a bit like pretzel sticks.**

📖 Invite everyone to eat a pretzel stick while you read Luke 2:8 aloud.

110   All Together Sunday School Book 1

With shepherds come sheep! Marshmallow sheep, to be exact! Put a handful of marshmallows in each person's cup. **The shepherds were watching their sheep when suddenly an angel appeared and said the words in today's Bible verses.**

I'll read the verses again. Be ready to toss a marshmallow into your mouth when you hear the words "great joy."

"I bring you good news that will bring great joy to all people. The Savior...has been born." Repeat several times, giving kids more chances to catch a marshmallow in their mouths. Welcome giggles and fun.

Everyone freeze! Stop munching for a bit. I have a question for you.

Ask: **How did eating marshmallows bring joy to our room?**

Say: **You may have been feeling sleepy, calm, silly, or even mad when we began the Bible story. Then poof! Food! Food is good at bringing joy and delight to people, no matter how they're feeling.**

Ask: **What other foods bring you joy?**

Say: **Marshmallows are great. But joy from Jesus is even better. Let's continue the story to find out why. On to the next Joy Mix ingredient—animal crackers!**

Add a few animal crackers to each person's cup. **After they heard the angel's message, the shepherds ran to Bethlehem to find Jesus. They wanted to see this Savior for themselves! Imagine their surprise when they found baby Jesus with the animals!**

Let's hear your animals. Make noises that sound like the animals in your cup. If your animal doesn't really make a noise, well, just make one up. Allow time, making some noises, too!

Jesus, the Savior—the Hero!—lay in a feeding trough. What an unexpected gift! Munch on a few animal crackers while we talk about this question:

Ask: **Tell about a time you received a gift you didn't expect. What was the gift? Did you like it?** Share an example from your own life to begin.

Say: **God's people expected a king, not a baby. They didn't know that this baby king would bring something even better than a country or new rules. <u>Jesus brings joy</u>.** *(It's true!)*

Let's keep eating this story! Next up, M&M's. Today that stands for Jesus' "mom, Mary." Put M&M's in each person's cup. **Jesus' mom, Mary, knew her baby boy was special. Listen to this.**

Read aloud Luke 2:17-19.

God had told Mary that her child was the hero people were looking for. She treasured what she knew in her heart. Maybe Mary treasured those first few hours with Jesus because she knew there would be a time she wouldn't be with him.

Lesson 9   111

Tell the Easter story.

You see, Jesus came to bring joy to all people—joy that comes from being close friends with God. Sin keeps people from being close to God. Sin causes people to hurt each other and make wrong choices. So Jesus came to save people from sin. He did that when he died on the cross. Let's use two pretzel sticks to make a cross shape. Allow time.

Jesus was put in a tomb after dying on a cross. A stone was rolled in front of the tomb. Imagine this cracker is a stone. Give each person a Ritz cracker. Have kids "roll" the crackers in front of their snack cups.

But the stone didn't stay there! The stone rolled away when Jesus came back to life again! Let's roll those crackers right into our mouths! Allow time.

That's **how Jesus brings joy. Jesus made a way for all people to be forgiven, forever friends with God. That friendship with God brings joy. No matter how we feel or what we're going through, we have joy because we have Jesus!**

Pray together.

Let's pray and thank Jesus for this food *and* for the gift of joy he brings. We usually pray before we eat. But today let's eat and pray at the same time! Be ready to eat each item I say as I pray.

Pray: **Dear Jesus, thank you for bringing joy to the world.**

As we eat a pretzel stick, we thank you for forgiving us and loving us no matter what. Pause to eat.

As we eat a marshmallow, we thank you for your sweet friendship. Pause to eat.

As we eat an animal cracker, we thank you for unexpected gifts we've received that bring us joy. Pause to eat.

And as we eat M&M's, our hearts treasure you. Pause to eat.

Ask the Prayer Person to pray a simple prayer or simply say "Amen!" Then let everyone enjoy the rest of their snack before moving on.

Wonder What Stations (15-20 minutes)

> Kids will wonder and wander their way through these three free-flowing application activities. Young kids may gravitate toward some things while older kids are drawn to others.

Say: Let's keep exploring Luke 2:10-11 with the items in this Wonder What Bin. You'll have three choices—I wonder what you'll choose to do first!

Dramatically re-reveal what's inside the Wonder What Bin, and explain these three different options for kids to choose during a free-play time. After 15-20 minutes, tell kids you'll be cleaning up the Wonder What Stations in about a minute. Have Happy Helpers return supplies to the Wonder What Bin.

Supplies:
- Wonder What Bin

Let's Play

Choose someone to hide a pompom in this room while others close their eyes. When ready, search for the pompom while the hider says if they're "hot" (close) or "cold" (far away).

Say: You guided your friends to the pompom, like the angels guided the shepherds to Jesus. The angels announced "good news that would bring great joy to all people." That good news was Jesus! Jesus brings joy. *(It's true!)*

Ask: What are some beautiful things you notice God creating in our world now?

Try This

Blow into a straw to make a bubble mountain! Place a cup on a serving tray (for easy cleanup), put a drop of dish soap in the cup, then add a little water. Blow out through the straw to create bubbles—don't breathe in this time! How big will the bubble mountain grow?

Say: Like a little soap creates a mountain of bubbles, remembering that Jesus brings joy can make a big difference in our lives. *(It's true!)*

Ask: What little reminder of Jesus' love has brought you a lot of joy this week?

As kids play, meander around the area, using these questions and comments to connect each activity to today's Bible verse and Bible Point.

Take a Look

Look through photos and find moments of joy.

Ask: How do people's faces look in these photos? What emotions might they be feeling in those moments of joy? Briefly tell about the photos and why they are important to you.

Say: Jesus brought joy to the shepherds that first Christmas. Jesus still brings joy to people's lives today. *(It's true!)*

Lesson 9

Review Together (5 minutes)

> Work together to create actions for words in the Bible verse.

Supplies:
- Here & Home papers (1 per child)
- crayons

Say: Spending time all together today has brought me joy. I'm so glad that we get to be friends with Jesus together.

Let's create some actions to do as we say Luke 2:10-11 all together. Rather than *me* telling you what to do, you kids can create the actions for us. You're in charge!

Invite kids to work together to make up actions for these words:

- good news
- great joy
- Savior
- born

Say Luke 2:10-11 together with actions:

"I bring you good news that will bring great joy to all people. The Savior…has been born."

Friendship with Jesus is a gift. That gift is from God to everyone who believes and trusts in Jesus. Jesus' friendship brings joy to our hearts because we know that no matter what happens or how we feel, God loves us, cares about us, and is always with us.

Jesus brings joy. *(It's true!)* And when you're friends with Jesus, he just might work through you to bring joy to others.

Take some time to affirm kids by name, thanking them for bringing you joy today.

Here & Home

Give kids each the Here & Home paper on page 115. Invite them to color and complete the Bible verse page now, and point out the activity for them to lead their parents in at home.

---

114   All Together Sunday School Book 1

Jesus Brings Joy

Here

Color the word "JOY." After you've colored each letter, jump like the person on the letter!

"I bring you good news that will bring great **JOY** to all people. The Savior...has been born."

Luke 2:10-11

Home

Jesus Brings Joy

"I bring you good news that will bring great joy to all people. The Savior...has been born" (Luke 2:10-11).

Have you ever felt like you should feel joy? Perhaps it's the Christmas season, and beautiful music, twinkling lights, and happy children are all around. But you feel sad. Or it's springtime! Flowers are blooming, birds are chirping, and your heart is breaking. In those moments, you may not feel joy. But, child of God, you still have it.

Search a dictionary and you'll see that the word *joy* has a variety of definitions, including "a source or cause of delight." For God's children, Jesus is the source of great joy. In other words, joy is a delightful gift from Jesus!

In Luke 2:10-11, the angel announced that joy had arrived because Jesus was born. When shepherds were scared, they had joy. When Joseph felt stress, he had joy. When Mary felt tired, she had joy. Why? Because Jesus was there. The Savior of the world had arrived. And he's still with people today—including your family.

Fun Fact
Contrary to cute Christmas pageant costumes, Luke 2 doesn't mention angels' halos or wings. But it was still an out-of-this world experience! Check out the details given as you reread Luke 2:9-14.

Read & Do
Read Luke 2:19. When you treasure something, you hold it lovingly in your heart. Find something in your home that you treasure. Show it to your family, and tell why you treasure it.

Think & Talk
Other than your friendship with Jesus, what's one thing that brought you joy today?

Say & Pray
Thank God for the things you treasure. Then thank God for sending Jesus—the greatest treasure of all!

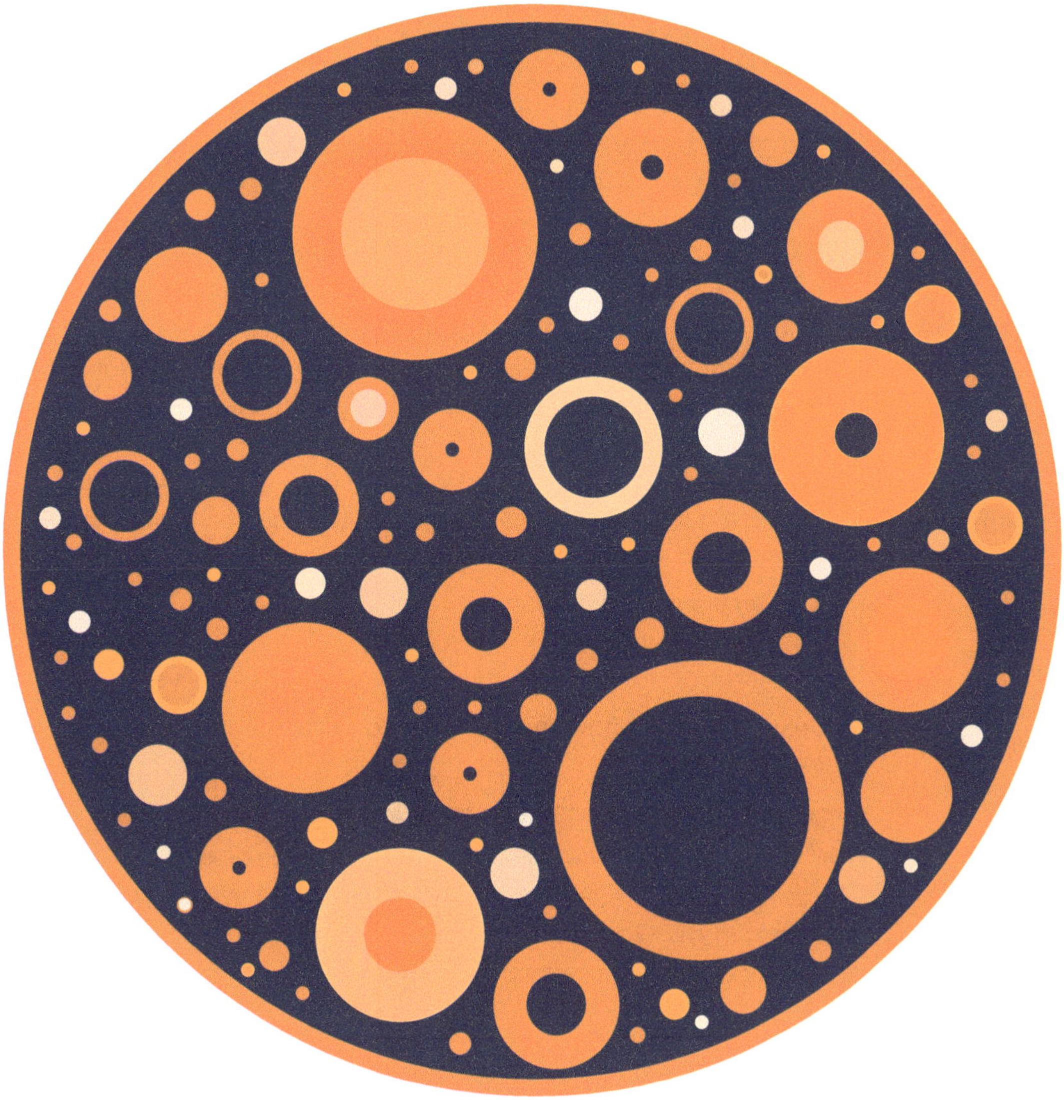

Lesson 10: Jesus Shows Us How to Love

"Love each other. Just as I have loved you, you should love each other" (John 13:34).

Discover John 13:34

Guess what! Jesus loves you. It's really true! You don't have to earn it or work hard to get it. Simply receive Jesus' out-of-this-world affection for you today, then get ready to share it.

The words in John 13:34 challenge Jesus' friends to not only enjoy his surprising love but also share it with each other.

On our own, we may not be able to muster up genuinely unselfish and loyal affection for others. So it's a good thing we have an example to follow! Jesus has shown the way, and he's with us, ready to let his love flow through us to our friends, family members, and everyone we meet. That includes the kids you'll lead today.

As you teach this lesson, you won't just talk about love. You'll create moments for kids to practice loving each other just as Jesus loves them. As they practice loving each other...

- Games will be more fun.
- Patience will come more naturally.
- And God's Word will come to life in practical ways.

Jesus shows us how to love. Look to Jesus' example as you lead and serve kids today.

PRAYER

Lord Jesus, you are in charge of this lesson. May your love be evident in my words and actions as I serve your children with humility and grace. Amen.

Fun Fact

In Bible times, dinner party hosts provided water for guests to wash their *own* feet. Foot washing was even too low for servants to do for others! Perhaps the host of the dinner Jesus and his friends attended before his death had forgotten to provide water, or maybe Jesus rewashed his friends' feet to demonstrate selfless love.

Lesson Overview

Bible Verse: John 13:34 | **Bible Point:** Jesus shows us how to love. *(It's true!)* | **Bible Exploration:** John 13:1-17, 33-35

Lesson-at-a-Glance

Play Together (10-15 minutes)
Kick a ball back and forth and/or become a cleaning crew.

Talk Together | Pray Together (10 minutes)
Talk about how you're feeling today, then pray and talk with God about it.

Bible Discovery (10-15 minutes)
Find and read John 13:34 together, gather for "supper," then draw feet and wash them.

Wonder What Stations (15-20 minutes)
Choose and move through the following activities:
- Create: Draw food your friends and family members love to eat.
- Imagine That: Build things with magnetic tiles or Legos.
- Let's Play: Make up a ball game that lovingly includes everyone.

Review Together (5 minutes)
Work together to create actions for words in the Bible verse, and give out Here & Home papers.

Supply List

- ☐ Bible bookmarked at John 13:34
- ☐ All Together Tasks labels (1 sheet for every 8 kids) (on page 8)
- ☐ Feelings Charts (1 for every 2 kids) (on page 9)
- ☐ crayons
- ☐ plastic tablecloth
- ☐ spray bottle with ¼ cup vinegar and 2½ cups water
- ☐ permanent markers
- ☐ Here & Home papers (1 per child) (on page 127)

Wonder What Bin Contents

- ☐ magnetic tiles or Legos
- ☐ paper plates
- ☐ washable markers
- ☐ paper towels
- ☐ foam balls or playground balls
- ☐ antibacterial wipes

The "Wonder What Bin"

This supply box is a key part of each All Together Sunday School lesson. This large container will store all the toys and supplies needed for the Play Together activities and Wonder What Stations. Each week, kids will "wonder what" is in store for them! Your Wonder What Bin could be a plastic storage bin, a treasure chest, a toy box, or any large container.

Lesson 10

All Together Tasks

Supplies: All Together Tasks labels (1 sheet for every 8 kids)

As kids arrive, explain the special jobs and encourage each child to choose one to do today. Download and print the All Together Tasks labels or copy them from page 8, and let kids choose the jobs they want to do. It's okay if more than one child has the same job or if one child has a few jobs. Teachers can have another job, too!

Kids choose from the following jobs:

Ready Reader is ready and willing to read a Bible verse aloud.

Prayer Person prays aloud nice and loud so everyone can hear.

Happy Helpers jump at the chance to hand out supplies and clean up stuff.

Befrienders are on the lookout for those who need help and support.

Greeters say, "Hello and welcome!" to everyone as they arrive and "Have a good day!" to everyone as they leave.

Play Together (10-15 minutes)

Play with the kids, using their favorite toys and games to help introduce the Bible Point. Choose one or both activities.

Supplies:
- Wonder What Bin

Foot Ball Fun

Gently kick a foam ball back and forth with a partner. How many times can you kick and receive the ball?

Ask: What sports or activities do people need to use their feet in?

Say: Feet come in handy! Today we'll hear about a time Jesus taught a lesson about love—using his friends' feet! Jesus kindly cared for others, and Jesus shows us how to love.

Cleaning Crew

Toys can get rather grimy and germy. So use antibacterial wipes to clean the magnetic tiles and Legos. Then work together to build something cool with the clean pieces.

Ask: What's something in your home you *don't* like to clean? Why is cleaning that thing so gross?

Say: Thank you, cleaning crew! Today we'll hear about how Jesus didn't mind cleaning in order to show true love in action. Jesus shows us how to love, too.

Talk Together (5 minutes)

> Kids talk in pairs about how they're feeling today.

Say: Today we'll talk with God and hear what God has to say to us through words in the Bible. But first, let's talk together. How are you feeling today?

Form pairs, and give each pair a Feelings Chart and a crayon. Have partners each circle the face that reflects how they're feeling in this moment and then tell their partners why they chose that face. Be sure to find a partner, too, and participate with the kids as they chat.

Pray Together (5 minutes)

> Kids tell God how they're feeling and pray a prayer all together.

Say: Thanks for talking with a friend! In the Bible, we read that we can pray and tell God anything. You'll see the words of that Bible verse printed on the Feelings Chart. If you'd like to read along, please do! Or you can simply listen as I read God's words.

Philippians 4:6 says, "Pray about everything. Tell God what you need, and thank him for all he has done."

Like we just talked with our friends, we can talk with God! Let's practice doing that now. We'll silently pray and tell God how we're feeling today. After our thinking prayer, we'll pray a special prayer all together.

Invite kids to get comfortable and close their eyes as they pray.

Pray: Dear God, we want to tell you how we feel today and why we feel that way. Pause for several moments of silent prayer. **Thanks for listening, God.**

Say: Now let's pray all together. We'll ask God to guide our time together today.

Watch and do what I do! After each sentence, I'll pause and we'll say the words "All together" together!

Pray: Dear God,

May we love [make the shape of a heart with your hands] **you and each other.** ("All together!")

May we listen [cup hand behind ear] **to you and each other.** ("All together!")

May we learn [point to brain] **about you and each other.** ("All together!")

May we laugh and have fun [high-five a friend] **with you and each other.** ("All together!")

Thanks for bringing us ("All together!") **today. Amen.**

Supplies:
- Feelings Charts (1 for every 2 kids)
- crayons

Download and print or make one copy of the Feelings Chart on page 9 for every two people. Instead of printing each week, consider placing the charts in plastic sheet protectors. Then kids can use dry-erase markers to mark how they're feeling. Simply clean off the markings for next week!

This prayer will set the tone for your time together each day. Each sentence helps to communicate the values in your classroom and invites God to help everyone do their part, no matter their age! When behavior challenges arise, you can guide kids back to this prayer to steer them toward loving behaviors.

Lesson 10   121

📖 Bible Discovery (15 minutes)

Find and read a verse together, explore its Bible context, and talk about stories in the Bible that reinforce the main idea of the verse.

Supplies:
- Bible bookmarked at John 13:34
- plastic tablecloth
- permanent markers
- spray bottle with ¼ cup vinegar and 2½ cups water
- Wonder What Bin

Find and read John 13:34.

Say: Let's hear a Bible verse that'll help us get to know God and his Son, Jesus, better. Today we'll explore John 13:34.
    The Bible is made up of Bible *books, chapters,* and *verses.* Chapters are longer and verses are shorter—usually about one sentence.
    Let's hear John 13:34. John is the book, "13" is the chapter, and "34" is the verse. Like many verses in the Bible, this one is something Jesus said.
    Invite the Ready Reader to read the verse from your marked Bible. Have everyone clap to thank the Ready Reader for reading.

Ask: What does this verse tell us about Jesus?

Say: Jesus loved his friends, and he wanted his friends to love others. Jesus gives us a good example to follow. Today we'll see how Jesus shows us how to love. That's our Bible Point today. So every time you hear the words "Jesus shows us how to love," give two thumbs up and say, "It's true!" To practice, repeat the Bible Point and response several times.
    Jesus said the words of the Bible verse to his friends while they ate a meal together.

Ask: Imagine we're planning a dinner party right now. Name three friends you'd like to invite.
    Share examples from your life to give kids some time to think. If you have a larger group of kids, invite kids to turn to someone beside them and name the friends they'd invite. If your group is small, give everyone a turn to list their friends. You could even pretend to write down the names, as if you're planning a guest list.

Set the table.

Say: This is shaping up to be a fun dinner party. Hold up the plastic tablecloth. **Let's spread out this tablecloth and imagine it's our dinner table.** Place the tablecloth on the floor. Have Happy Helpers get paper plates from the Wonder What Bin to set around the "table." As they set the table, talk about this question.

Ask: What's fun about having friends or family members over for dinner?

Say: Sometimes it's just nice to be in a room filled with people we love. Invite everyone to gather and sit around the tablecloth. Make sure Befrienders are close to friends who may need some extra help.

122 All Together Sunday School Book 1

Before he said the words in John 13:34, Jesus gathered in a room with his closest friends, called the disciples. They were cozy and seated together—like we are now. Listen while I read what Jesus did to show love to his friends.

Read aloud John 13:4-5.

You heard that right. Jesus washed their feet! Back then roads were made of dirt, and people didn't wear tennis shoes or boots. So people's feet got pretty gross and dirty. Even servants who did a lot of hard—maybe even icky—jobs didn't wash other people's feet! But Jesus did. Because Jesus wanted to show his friends what it looks like to love and put others first.

Draw and wash feet.

Since our shoes are happy on our feet right now, let's not wash our feet. Instead, let's draw footprints on the tablecloth. Use a permanent marker to draw a footprint as an example. **We'll use permanent markers, so be very careful. Befrienders, be ready to help friends carefully draw feet.**

Collect the permanent markers and tuck them away. Have the Happy Helper put washable markers from the Wonder What Bin in the center of the tablecloth.

These feet look too clean. Let's use washable markers to make them dirty! Encourage kids to scribble over their feet drawings, then collect washable markers and return them to the Wonder What Bin.

Just look at these dirty feet! If they were real feet, how might they smell? Invite reactions. Then show the spray bottle and gently spray the feet drawings with the vinegar and water solution.

Do you smell something? It's vinegar!

Ask: What do you think vinegar smells like?

Say: **Vinegar may not be your favorite smell. But it does help make things clean. Let's keep reading what happened at Jesus' dinner party. He was washing feet, and he came to his friend Peter.**

Read aloud John 13:6-8.

Let's put ourselves in Peter's shoes—or sandals—for a moment. Think of your best friend. Say that person's name on the count of three. 1, 2, 3! Invite kids' responses.

Ask: How would you feel if your best friend tried to wash your feet while you were having dinner?

Say: **Seems like Peter was a little surprised and grossed out, too. Wasn't his best friend, Jesus, too important to wash feet?**

But Jesus was making a point. *No one* **is too special or important to serve others. Jesus was God's Son! And yet he was willing to get his hands dirty in order to show his friends what love looks like.**

Encourage kids to draw feet rather than trace their shoes. That way, shoes won't get marked up by markers.

Lesson 10   123

Let's follow Jesus' example and wash these feet! Give everyone a paper towel from the Wonder What Bin, and show them how to wipe off the marker scribbles. Be ready to spray a little more vinegar water when needed. Once feet are clean, have Happy Helpers collect and throw away paper towels.

That foot-washing fun happened right before Jesus said the words in today's Bible verse. Listen while I read John 13:34 again.

"Love each other. Just as I have loved you, you should love each other."

Jesus loved his friends. He served his friends. And he was about to give up his life in order to make a way for all his friends to become forgiven and forever friends with God—that includes you and me! If you have a small group, mention each child by name: "That includes you, David, and you, Melody, and you, Cassie, and me, too."

It's not always easy to love our friends and family. Sometimes they get on our nerves. We might want to put ourselves and what *we* want first instead of putting them first. But Jesus will help us follow his example. <u>Jesus shows us how to love</u>. *(It's true!)*

Pray together.

Let's pray and ask Jesus to help us follow in his loving steps. Everyone, please stand on the footprints you drew. They're nice and clean now! Allow time.

I'll pray. When you hear me say "switch," you'll lovingly and carefully move one foot so you are standing on someone else's footprint. You might have to work together to figure out where to stand—and that's okay. This little move will give you a chance to practice loving others. Here we go!

Pray: **Dear Jesus, hearing stories about your time on earth helps us see how loving and kind you are. Thanks for this story of when you washed your friends' feet. Even though we can't see you anymore, we know you are with us and will help us love others. Help us right now as we...**

Switch! Allow time for kids to lovingly work together so everyone can stand on a different footprint.

Jesus, with your help, may we keep loving others like you love us.

Ask the Prayer Person to pray a simple prayer or simply say "Amen!"

Wonder What Stations (15-20 minutes)

> Kids will wonder and wander their way through these three free-flowing application activities. Young kids may gravitate toward some things while older kids are drawn to others.

Say: Let's keep exploring John 13:34 with the items in this Wonder What Bin. You'll have three choices—I wonder what you'll choose to do first!

Supplies:
- Wonder What Bin

Dramatically re-reveal what's inside the Wonder What Bin, and explain these three different options for kids to choose during a free-play time. After 15-20 minutes, tell kids you'll be cleaning up the Wonder What Stations in about a minute. Have Happy Helpers return supplies to the Wonder What Bin.

Create

Think of people you love. If you were to make a special meal to show them you love them, what food would you prepare? Use markers to draw the food on a paper plate.

Ask: How could you help someone prepare food for your family this week? What are things you can do to help show Jesus' love to your grown-ups?

Say: Jesus shows us how to love. *(It's true!)* **Jesus served his friends by washing their feet. We can serve our friends and family members, too!**

Let's Play

Form a circle. Toss, roll, or tap the ball to different people around the circle. Change the way you move the ball based on the person you're passing it to. For example, you might roll it to a younger child who struggles to catch the ball. Or you might toss the ball harder to an older friend who needs a challenge. Show love to each other in the way you move the ball across the circle.

Say: As you moved the ball around the circle, you followed Jesus' example and put others' needs before your own. Jesus shows us how to love. *(It's true!)* **Way to practice loving each other well!**

As kids play, meander around the area, using these questions and comments to connect each activity to today's Bible verse and Bible Point.

Ask: Who is good at showing Jesus' love to you? It could be a family member, a teacher, or a friend!

Imagine That

Build cool things with magnetic tiles or Legos.

Say: If we look up the word *love*, one definition is a "warm attachment." When things are attached, they stick together!

Ask: How would *you* describe love?

Lesson 10

Review Together (5 minutes)

> Work together to create actions for words in the Bible verse.

Supplies:
- Here & Home papers (1 per child)
- crayons

Say: You know, Jesus is God's Son, and there is no one like him. But because Jesus became human and lived on earth for a while, he does have a few things in common with us.

For example, Jesus' feet got dirty, and so do ours. Jesus loved his friends just like we love ours. And we can be ready to show love to new friends, too.

Let's create some actions to do as we say John 13:34 all together. Rather than *me* telling you what to do, you kids can create the actions for us. You're in charge!

Invite kids to work together to make up actions for these words:

- Love
- each other
- I
- you

Say John 13:34 together with actions:
"Love each other. Just as I have loved you, you should love each other."

<u>Jesus shows us how to love.</u> *(It's true!)* We don't have to wash our friends' feet in order to love like Jesus. But we can do selfless things like letting people go first when we play a game or putting family members' toys—or even shoes—away for them.

Ask: What other things can we do to show friends and family members that we love them?

Say: Those are great ideas! Have some fun watching for ways you can show Jesus' love this week. And have joy remembering just how much Jesus loves you. He gave up everything—including his life—to show how much God loves people—and that includes you.

Take some time to affirm kids by name, saying: **Jesus loves you, [child's name].**

Here & Home

Give kids each the Here & Home paper on page 127. Invite them to color and complete the Bible verse page now, and point out the activity for them to lead their parents in at home.

Jesus Shows Us How to Love

Here

Color the words in the Bible verse in a fun way. You could make patterns with dots, lines, or squiggles. Show love to friends by telling what you like about their artwork. Share your ideas with friends to give them ideas for their work of art, too!

JOHN 13:34 LOVE EACH OTHER. JUST AS I HAVE LOVED YOU, YOU SHOULD LOVE EACH OTHER.

Permission to copy this resource from All Together Sunday School granted for local church use.
Copyright © 2024 Group Publishing, Inc., Loveland, CO. group.com

Home

Jesus Shows Us How to Love

"Love each other. Just as I have loved you, you should love each other" (John 13:34).

How did Jesus show his love for you today? Was it through a friend's kindness? Did you feel his love through a big hug? Did words in the Bible bring comfort and peace to your heart?

Jesus loves you. It's true! Enjoy Jesus' out-of-this-world affection. Let Jesus love you so you're ready to love, too.

John 13:34 challenges Jesus' friends to not only enjoy his love but also share this love with each other. Love is more than a feeling—it's a choice. On our own, we may not be able to show unselfish and loyal affection for others. Good thing we have an example to follow! Jesus has shown the way, and he's with us, ready to let his love flow through us to our friends, family members, and everyone we meet. That includes the people in your family.

Fun Fact

In Bible times, dinner party hosts provided water for guests to wash their own feet. Foot washing was even too low for servants to do for others! Perhaps the host of the dinner Jesus and his friends attended before his death had forgotten to provide water, or maybe Jesus rewashed his friends' feet in order to demonstrate selfless love.

Read & Do

Read John 13:34. Then hug each person in your family and say, "I love you."

Think & Talk

What's one thing you love about each person in your family? Tell them!

Say & Pray

Sit or stand in a circle. Choose someone to begin praying and pray for the person to the right. Continue until each person in your family has been prayed for.

Lesson 10

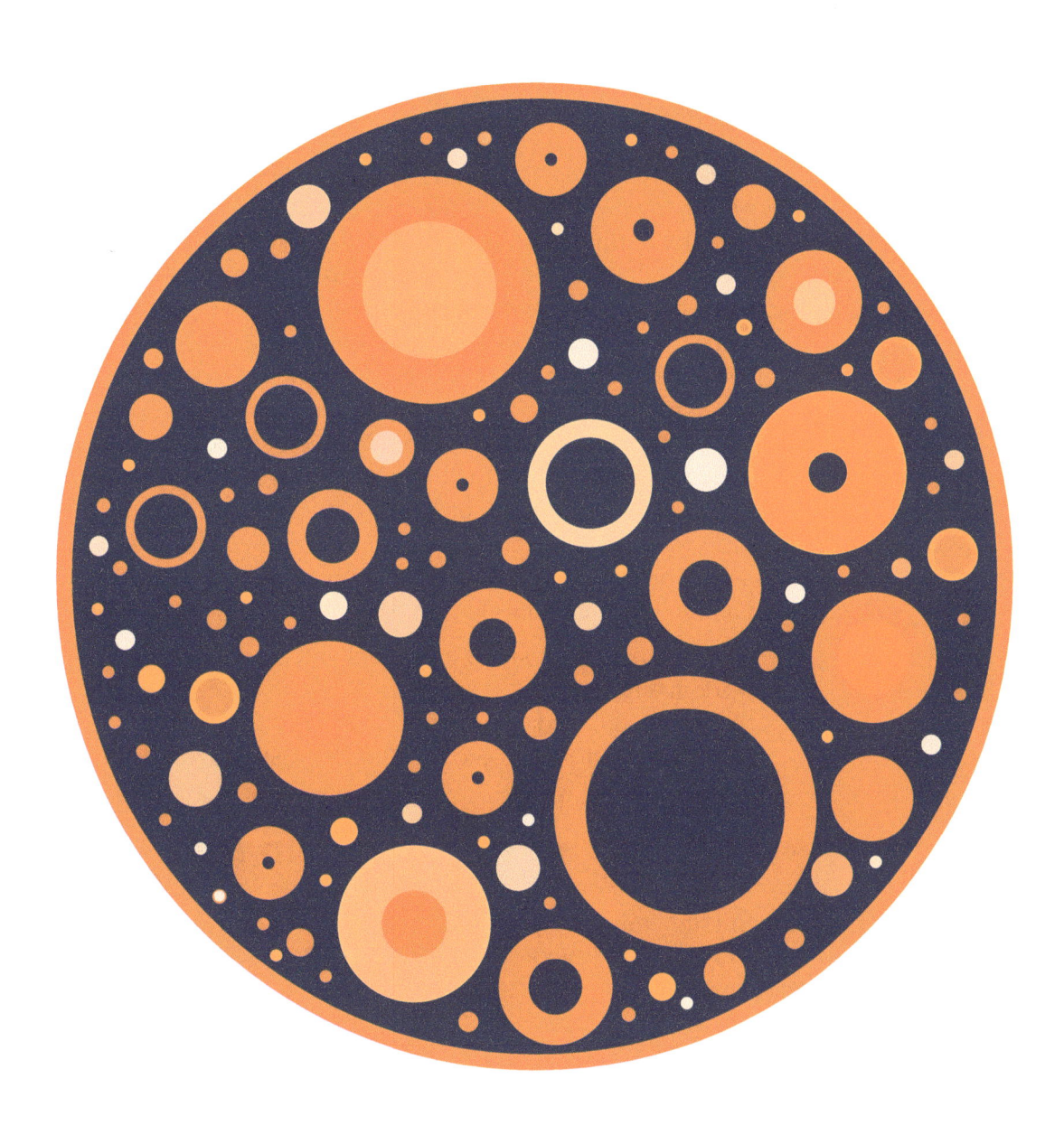

Lesson 11: The Holy Spirit Gives Us Power

"But you will receive power when the Holy Spirit comes upon you" (Acts 1:8).

Discover Acts 1:8

The lights flicker a few times, then it happens. The power goes out. No electricity means no watching TV. You can't charge your phone. Vacuuming has to wait. The refrigerator stops cooling. Appliances cease all operations. If it's nighttime, you can't even see well enough to play a board game.

Sigh. You don't realize how much you rely on power until it's gone.

Thankfully, when it comes to living as a child of God, you will never find yourself powerless. In Acts 1:8, Jesus promises power from the Holy Spirit. This divine power would help his friends go and tell the world the good news: through Jesus, there is a way to become forgiven and forever friends with God.

Even today, the Holy Spirit fills us with the power we need to trust Jesus and live in a way that welcomes others to befriend Jesus and become part of God's family, too.

The Holy Spirit gives us power. So, fueled by that divine strength, you're charged and ready to lead this lesson. The Holy Spirit will empower you to...

- Think fast and respond to behaviors and comments with wisdom and love.
- Move with kids and join the fun.
- Teach with confidence and trust the Holy Spirit's guidance.

You have the power to be Jesus' witness in your classroom today.

PRAYER

Holy Spirit, I welcome you to this classroom today. Empower me to teach, reach, and love your children well today. In Jesus' name, amen.

Fun Fact

The word *apostle* comes from the verb "to send out." In the New Testament, the word *apostle* usually refers to someone who knew Jesus and was personally sent out by him.

Lesson Overview

✝ **Bible Verse:** Acts 1:8 | **Bible Point:** The Holy Spirit gives us power. *(It's true!)* | **Bible Exploration:** Acts 1:1-8; 2:1-12

Lesson-at-a-Glance

Play Together (10-15 minutes)
Use a fan to make a balloon float in the air and/or create a workout program.

Talk Together | Pray Together (10 minutes)
Talk about how you're feeling today, then pray and talk with God about it.

Bible Discovery (10-15 minutes)
Find and read Acts 1:8 together, and make and tell a Bible story with ping-pong people.

Wonder What Stations (15-20 minutes)
Choose and move through the following activities:
- Take a Look: Look at world maps and Bibles printed in different languages.
- Let's Play: Play Musical Chairs.
- Create: Draw on balloons, then fill them with air.

Review Together (5 minutes)
Work together to create actions for words in the Bible verse, and give out Here & Home papers.

Supply List

- ☐ Bible bookmarked at Acts 1:8
- ☐ All Together Tasks labels (1 sheet for every 8 kids) (on page 8)
- ☐ Feelings Charts (1 for every 2 kids) (on page 9)
- ☐ crayons
- ☐ Here & Home papers (1 per child) (on page 139)
- ☐ ping-pong balls (2 per child)
- ☐ container to hold ping-pong balls
- ☐ smiley face stickers
- ☐ chairs (enough to play Musical Chairs)

Wonder What Bin Contents

- ☐ adjustable fan that tilts up
- ☐ balloons
- ☐ balloon pump *(optional)*
- ☐ world maps and Bible-times maps
- ☐ Bibles printed in different languages
- ☐ permanent markers
- ☐ music player
- ☐ upbeat music

The "Wonder What Bin"

This supply box is a key part of each All Together Sunday School lesson. This large container will store all the toys and supplies needed for the Play Together activities and Wonder What Stations. Each week, kids will "wonder what" is in store for them! Your Wonder What Bin could be a plastic storage bin, a treasure chest, a toy box, or any large container.

Lesson 11   131

All Together Tasks

Supplies: All Together Tasks labels (1 sheet for every 8 kids)

As kids arrive, explain the special jobs and encourage each child to choose one to do today. Download and print the All Together Tasks labels or copy them from page 8, and let kids choose the jobs they want to do. It's okay if more than one child has the same job or if one child has a few jobs. Teachers can have another job, too!

Kids choose from the following jobs:

Ready Reader is ready and willing to read a Bible verse aloud.

Prayer Person prays aloud nice and loud so everyone can hear.

Happy Helpers jump at the chance to hand out supplies and clean up stuff.

Befrienders are on the lookout for those who need help and support.

Greeters say, "Hello and welcome!" to everyone as they arrive and "Have a good day!" to everyone as they leave.

Play Together (10-15 minutes)

Play with the kids, using their favorite toys and games to help introduce the Bible Point. Choose one or both activities.

Supplies:
- Wonder What Bin

Hover Balloon

Plug in the fan, then tilt it so the air blows straight up. Inflate a few balloons and tie them off. Turn on the fan. How many balloons can hover above the fan at once?

Ask: What makes this activity fun? What's frustrating about it?

Say: Through the fan's power, balloons hovered in the air! And through the Holy Spirit's power, Jesus' friends can do some pretty cool things, too. The Holy Spirit gives us power.

Workout!

Imagine you're in a workout class. Choose someone to be the instructor. That person will make up exercises (like jumping jacks, squats, and marching in place) and show everyone what to do. Play upbeat music as you work out together. After a few minutes, choose a new leader.

Ask: What do you like about exercising?

Say: Workouts help people stay healthy and strong. Today we'll hear a Bible verse that talks about power that doesn't come from a good workout. It comes from the Holy Spirit. The Holy Spirit gives us power.

Talk Together (5 minutes)

> Kids talk in pairs about how they're feeling today.

Say: Today we'll talk with God and hear what God has to say to us through words in the Bible. But first, let's talk together. How are you feeling today?

Form pairs, and give each pair a Feelings Chart and a crayon. Have partners each circle the face that reflects how they're feeling in this moment and then tell their partners why they chose that face. Be sure to find a partner, too, and participate with the kids as they chat.

Supplies:
- Feelings Charts (1 for every 2 kids)
- crayons

Download and print or make one copy of the Feelings Chart on page 9 for every two people. Instead of printing each week, consider placing the charts in plastic sheet protectors. Then kids can use dry-erase markers to mark how they're feeling. Simply clean off the markings for next week!

Pray Together (5 minutes)

> Kids tell God how they're feeling and pray a prayer all together.

Say: Thanks for talking with a friend! In the Bible, we read that we can pray and tell God anything. You'll see the words of that Bible verse printed on the Feelings Chart. If you'd like to read along, please do! Or you can simply listen as I read God's words.

Philippians 4:6 says, "Pray about everything. Tell God what you need, and thank him for all he has done."

Like we just talked with our friends, we can talk with God! Let's practice doing that now. We'll silently pray and tell God how we're feeling today. After our thinking prayer, we'll pray a special prayer all together.

Invite kids to get comfortable and close their eyes as they pray.

Pray: Dear God, we want to tell you how we feel today and why we feel that way. Pause for several moments of silent prayer. Thanks for listening, God.

Say: Now let's pray all together. We'll ask God to guide our time together today.

Watch and do what I do! After each sentence, I'll pause and we'll say the words "All together" together!

Pray: Dear God,

> **May we love** [make the shape of a heart with your hands] **you and each other.** ("All together!")
>
> **May we listen** [cup hand behind ear] **to you and each other.** ("All together!")
>
> **May we learn** [point to brain] **about you and each other.** ("All together!")
>
> **May we laugh and have fun** [high-five a friend] **with you and each other.** ("All together!")
>
> **Thanks for bringing us** ("All together!") **today. Amen.**

This prayer will set the tone for your time together each day. Each sentence helps to communicate the values in your classroom and invites God to help everyone do their part, no matter their age! When behavior challenges arise, you can guide kids back to this prayer to steer them toward loving behaviors.

📖 Bible Discovery (15 minutes)

Find and read a verse together, explore its Bible context, and talk about stories in the Bible that reinforce the main idea of the verse.

Supplies:
- Bible bookmarked at Acts 1:8
- container of ping-pong balls
- smiley face stickers

Find and read Acts 1:8.

Say: **Let's hear a Bible verse that'll help us get to know God even better. Today we'll explore Acts 1:8.**

The Bible is divided into two parts: the Old Testament and the New Testament. Acts is in the New Testament of the Bible. It tells about the first Christians. Let's hear Acts 1:8.

Invite the Ready Reader to read the verse from your marked Bible. Have everyone clap to thank the Ready Reader for reading.

You might hear that verse and wonder, "Who is the Holy Spirit?" Well, the Holy Spirit is God. Our one true God is shown in three persons. When people talk about the Trinity, they're talking about God the Father, God the Son, and God the Holy Spirit.

It's a little hard to understand, isn't it?

In this verse, God the Son—that's Jesus—is talking about God the Holy Spirit. Jesus promised that even after he went back to heaven, God would still be with them because the Holy Spirit would come.

Whew! Listen to part of the verse again. "But you will receive power when the Holy Spirit comes upon you."

Ask: **What does this verse tell us about the Holy Spirit?**

Say: **This verse tells us that <u>the Holy Spirit gives us power</u>! That's our Bible Point today. So every time you hear the words "The Holy Spirit gives us power," give two thumbs up and say, "It's true!"** To practice, repeat the Bible Point and response several times.

Bounce a ping-pong ball.

Have everyone sit in a circle on the floor. Bring the container of ping-pong balls and smiley face stickers with you. Make sure your circle is several feet away from an unobstructed wall. You'll be bouncing ping-pong balls to the wall.

Today's story begins after Jesus died on a cross and came back to life again. Jesus was gone, but then he came back. It was kind of like a bounce back! Toss or roll a ping-pong ball so it hits a wall and then bounces back. **Jesus was gone, but then he came back.** Give everyone a turn to toss a ping-pong ball against the wall, then put the balls back in the container.

Think of a time someone went away but then came back. Maybe a friend moved away but then came back for a visit. Or maybe you weren't in the same class as a friend one year in school, but the next year you were back together!

134 All Together Sunday School Book 1

Ask: Who went away and came back?

Ask: How did you feel to have that person back?

Say: Jesus' friends must have been happy to have him back. Jesus would pop in to see them every now and then.

📖 Read aloud Acts 1:3.

The apostles were Jesus' friends. They're also called "disciples" in the Bible because they followed Jesus and learned from him. But now, in the Bible book of Acts, they are called "apostles." That's a lot of words that can refer to "friends."

Ask: What other words do you use for "friend"?

Say: You call your friends different things, too! Well, the word *apostle* means "someone who is sent." Jesus' friends were about to be sent on a very special mission.

Make ping-pong people.

Hold up the ping-pong balls. **Let's imagine these ping-pong balls are the apostles. Some of their names were Peter, John, James, and Matthew! They're about to be sent out to tell about Jesus and help other people become his friends, too. Before they go, let's give them faces.** Invite each child to choose one ping-pong ball and place a smiley face sticker on the ball.

Now put your ping-pong person on your lap, and let's all turn so we're facing the wall. It's not time for the apostles to go out just yet, so keep them as still as you can. Allow time.

📖 Read aloud Acts 1:8.

Jesus said the Holy Spirit would give the apostles the power they needed to go and tell others about Jesus. Once the others heard about Jesus, they could become his friends, too!

After Jesus said this, he went back to heaven. Have everyone look up and wave goodbye with their ping-pong people in their hands. **Jesus left, and his friends never saw his body again. But they weren't all alone—God, the Holy Spirit was coming!**

Later, all Jesus' friends were meeting together—not just the apostles. Let's add more ping-pong people to the group. Allow time for kids to each add another smiley face to a different ping-pong ball and hold it in their other hand.

Turn on the fan, but point it away from the ping-pong balls. **Suddenly they heard wind! And they saw fire that didn't hurt anyone. All the believers were filled with the Holy Spirit, and they began speaking in different languages.**

Ask: Do you know how to say "hello" in another language? Invite kids to respond in languages they know, and repeat their responses. Share any greetings in other languages that you know. Then turn off the fan.

Say: Jesus' friends were filled with the Holy Spirit, and now they could talk to people from different places. They had God's power, so now it was time to go. Have everyone lie on the floor and gently blow on their ping-pong balls so they move toward the wall. Have kids try to get the balls to the wall without the balls bouncing back.

Like the air from our mouths powered the ping-pong balls, the Holy Spirit empowered Jesus' friends! The Holy Spirit guided them in telling about Jesus and helping others become his friends, too. We couldn't actually see the air that moved our ping-pong people, but we could see what it did. That's like the Holy Spirit! We can't see the Holy Spirit, but we see how the Holy Spirit empowers people.

Have kids go get their ping-pong balls.

Let's imagine these ping-pong people are Jesus' friends today—they are you and me and other people we know who love and follow Jesus. The Holy Spirit still gives the power we need to tell people about Jesus and help them become his friends, too.

Ask: Where will you go later today? Invite responses and choose one place.

Say: Imagine the wall is [the place you chose]**. The Holy Spirit gives us the power we need to live for Jesus there.** Have kids blow their ping-pong balls to the wall again, then bring them back to the starting point.

Ask: Where will you go later this week? Invite responses and choose one place.

Say: Imagine the wall is [the place you chose]**. The Holy Spirit gives us the power we need to live for Jesus there, too.** Have kids blow their ping-pong balls to the wall again, then bring them back to the starting point. Repeat as time allows, inviting kids to imagine the wall represents places they go.

As you go, you aren't alone. The Holy Spirit will give you the power you need to go where you need to go and do what you need to do. The Holy Spirit just may work through you to help people meet and become friends with Jesus.

Pray together.

Sit together in a circle again. **Let's pray and thank God, the Holy Spirit, for giving us power.**

Pray: Holy Spirit, you fill us with power. As we go different places and do different things, help us rely on you so we can invite people to become friends with Jesus and be part of God's family. Thank you.

Ask the Prayer Person to pray a simple prayer or simply say "Amen!"

Wonder What Stations (15-20 minutes)

> Kids will wonder and wander their way through these three free-flowing application activities. Young kids may gravitate toward some things while older kids are drawn to others.

Say: Let's keep exploring Acts 1:8 with the items in this Wonder What Bin. You'll have three choices—I wonder what you'll choose to do first!

Dramatically re-reveal what's inside the Wonder What Bin, and explain these three different options for kids to choose during a free-play time. After 15-20 minutes, tell kids you'll be cleaning up the Wonder What Stations in about a minute. Have Happy Helpers return supplies to the Wonder What Bin.

Supplies:
- Wonder What Bin

Take a Look

Look through world maps, Bible-times maps, and Bibles printed in different languages.

Ask: Where in the world do you want to go someday? What languages do you hope to learn and speak?

Say: Just think, the Holy Spirit still helps Jesus' friends share the good news of Jesus in all the different languages and places. How cool is that? The Holy Spirit gives us power. *(It's true!)*

Let's Play

Play Musical Chairs. Form a circle of chairs, with one less chair than the number of people playing. (Choose someone to start and stop the music, too.) When music plays, everyone will move around the inside of the chair circle. When it stops, they must rush to find a seat. The person who doesn't get a chair is out. Continue playing, removing a chair each round.

Ask: What would this game have been like with no music?

Say: The music powered this game! It told you when to go and when to stop. That's similar to the Holy Spirit. The Holy Spirit gives us power. *(It's true!)* Share an example from your own life. Perhaps the Holy Spirit helped you know what to say to a friend or cautioned you to think before acting on a feeling.

As kids play, meander around the area, using these questions and comments to connect each activity to today's Bible verse and Bible Point.

Try This

Write your name or draw your face on a balloon. Then inflate it and watch it grow. If you'd like, put it over the fan again to watch it soar!

Say: We don't have to do big stuff on our own. The Holy Spirit fills us with power to help us. The Holy Spirit gives us power. *(It's true!)*

Ask: What big stuff do you hope to do someday?

Lesson 11   137

Review Together (5 minutes)

> Work together to create actions for words in the Bible verse.

Supplies:
- Here & Home papers (1 per child)
- crayons

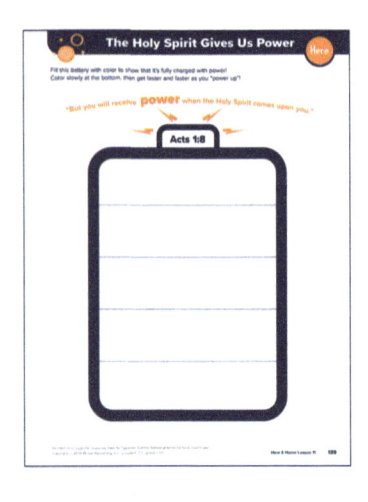

Say: Let's power up and invent some actions to do as we say Acts 1:8 all together. Rather than *me* **telling you what to do, you kids can create the actions for us. You're in charge!**

Invite kids to work together to make up actions for these words:

- you
- power
- Holy Spirit
- comes upon you

Say Acts 1:8 together with actions:
"But you will receive power when the Holy Spirit comes upon you."

**It's good to know that we don't need to muster up power to live for Jesus on our own. The Holy Spirit guides us, helps us, and gives us the strength we need.
The Holy Spirit gives us power.** *(It's true!)* **The Holy Spirit never goes away. When we feel stuck or tired, the Holy Spirit is with us, ready to give us power to keep trusting and following Jesus.**

Take some time to affirm kids by name, saying: [Child's name], **the Holy Spirit gives you power.**

Here & Home

Give kids each the Here & Home paper on page 139. Invite them to color and complete the Bible verse page now, and point out the activity for them to lead their parents in at home.

The Holy Spirit Gives Us Power

Here

Fill this battery with color to show that it's fully charged with power!
Color slowly at the bottom, then get faster and faster as you "power up"!

"But you will receive **power** when the Holy Spirit comes upon you."

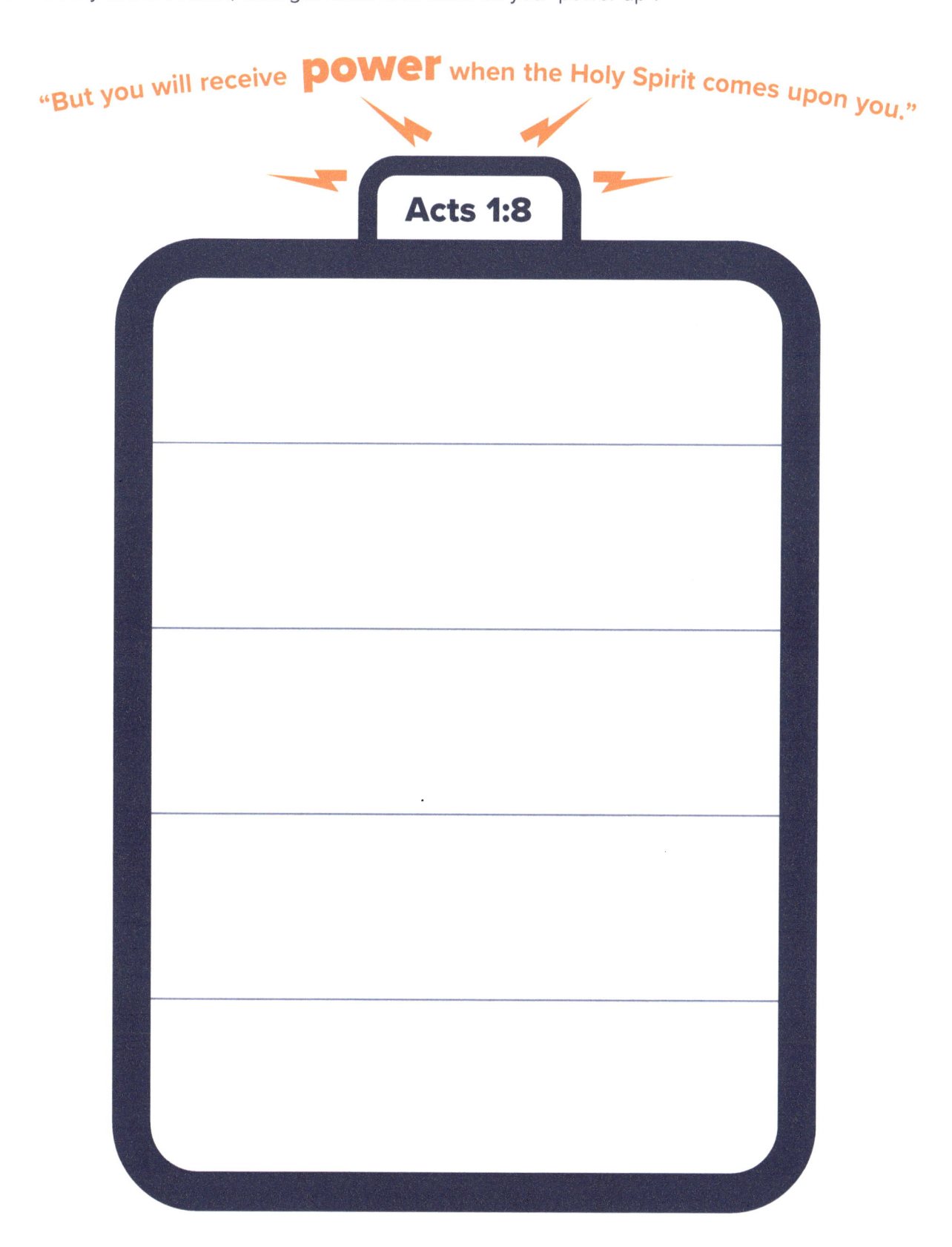

Acts 1:8

Permission to copy this resource from All Together Sunday School granted for local church use.
Copyright © 2024 Group Publishing, Inc., Loveland, CO. group.com

Here & Home Lesson 11

Home

The Holy Spirit Gives Us Power

"But you will receive power when the Holy Spirit comes upon you" (Acts 1:8).

The lights flicker a few times, then it happens. The power goes out. No electricity means no watching TV. No charging your phone. Vacuuming has to wait. The refrigerator stops cooling. Appliances cease all operations. If it's nighttime, you can't even see well enough to play a board game.

Sigh. You never know how much you rely on power until it's gone.

Thankfully, when it comes to living as a child of God, you will never find yourself powerless. In Acts 1:8, Jesus promises power from the Holy Spirit. This divine power would help his friends go and tell the world the good news: through Jesus, there is a way to become forgiven and forever friends with God.

Even today, the Holy Spirit fills your family with the power you need to trust Jesus and welcome others to become part of God's family, too.

Even during power outages, your family has the strength you need to live for Jesus.

Fun Fact

The word *apostle* comes from the verb "to send out." In the New Testament, the word *apostle* usually refers to someone who knew Jesus and was personally sent out by him.

Think & Talk

Who did you spend time with today? How might they have felt Jesus' love as they played or worked with you?

Read & Do

Read all the details about the Holy Spirit coming in Acts 2:1-12, and take turns telling your favorite part or wondering about something that happened.

Say & Pray

Think of people you know who haven't become friends with Jesus yet. Write their names, then pray for each person by name. Ask the Holy Spirit to help you know how to help those people meet and become forgiven and forever friends with Jesus.

Lesson 11

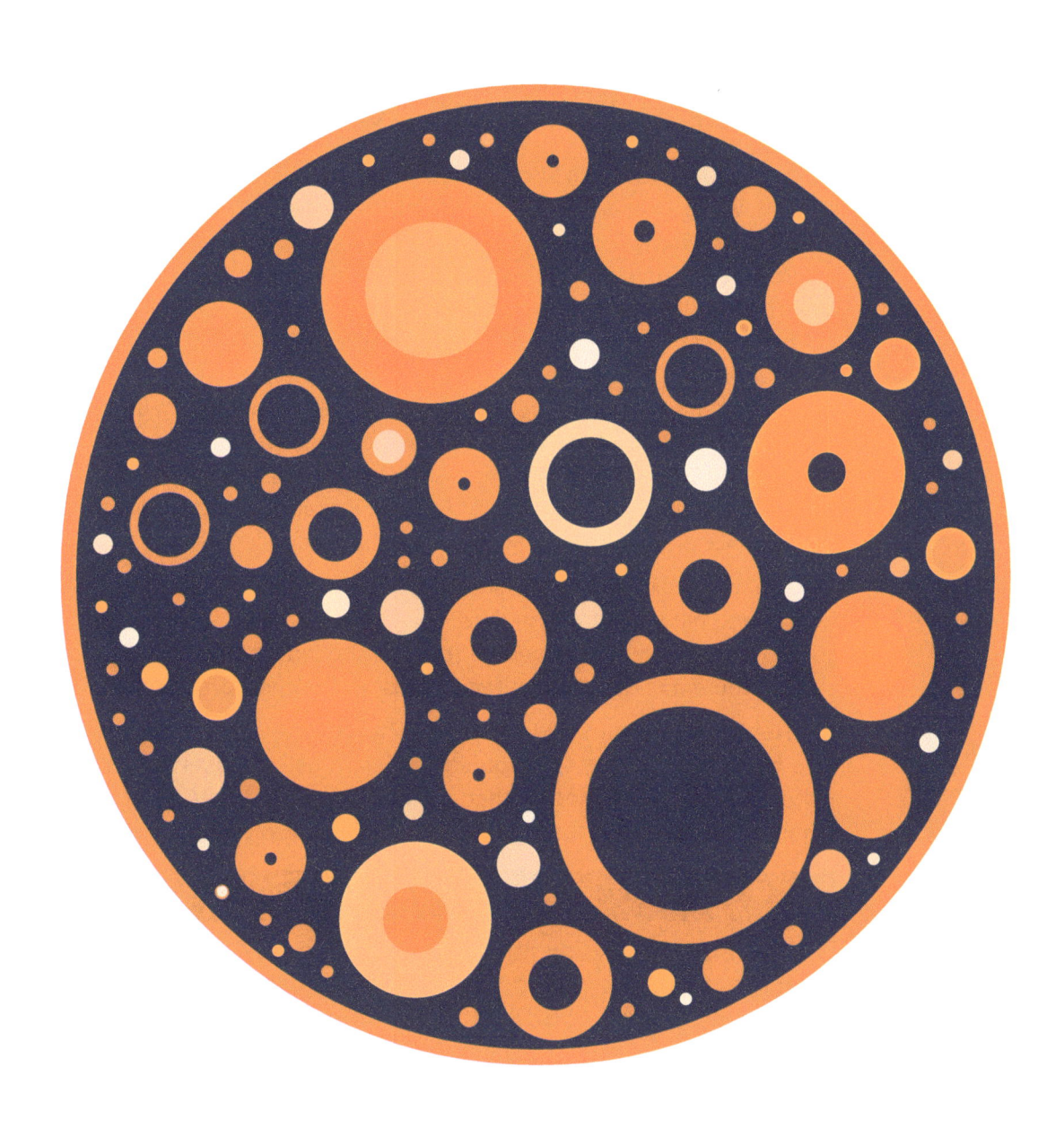

Lesson 12: Jesus Saves Us

"If you openly declare that Jesus is Lord and believe in your heart that God raised him from the dead, you will be saved" (Romans 10:9).

Discover Romans 10:9

"Nobody's perfect." It's a short sentence with a lot of truth. Try as we might, humans won't always say the right thing or do the right thing. We're bound to do and say "wrong."

But there's hope. Notice what Paul *doesn't* write in Romans 10:9. He doesn't say, "If you try hard to be perfect and never do anything wrong, you will be saved." He doesn't even state, "If you're good most of the time and only mess up a little, you will be saved."

Instead, Paul points to Jesus. To paraphrase his words, "When we say we belong to Jesus and believe he beat sin and death, then we are saved."

Jesus saves. He saves us from sin and death *and* from the pressure we put on ourselves to be God's perfect children. Because of Jesus, we're part of God's family and we're dearly loved—mistakes and all.

You may make some mistakes as you teach this lesson.
- You may lose track of time.
- You may not have perfect reactions to kids' behaviors.
- You may need to admit mess-ups and ask for forgiveness.

That's okay because Jesus saves. The best way to teach this truth to kids is to believe it and live it for yourself. Kids are astute observers. They learn behaviors even more deeply than what they're told. When you authentically embrace Jesus' grace for you, you'll show kids how to do the same!

Fun Fact

Did you know that in Romans 10, Paul rewrote words that Moses said to the Israelites in Deuteronomy 30:14? Moses told the Israelites that this message from God was "on your lips and in your heart so that you can obey it." Paul's message about Jesus was said with mouths and believed in hearts, too!

PRAYER

Dear Jesus, thank you for saving me. Help me view myself through the lens of your love and grace—not as a defective person but as a dearly loved child of God. Thank you. Amen.

Lesson Overview

Bible Verse: Romans 10:9 | **Bible Point:** Jesus saves us. *(It's true!)* | **Bible Exploration:** Romans 10:9; Luke 24:1-7

Lesson-at-a-Glance

Play Together (10-15 minutes)
Move across the room on pool noodle rings and/or play Simon Says.

Talk Together | Pray Together (10 minutes)
Talk about how you're feeling today, then pray and talk with God about it.

Bible Discovery (10-15 minutes)
Find and read Romans 10:9 together, shape chenille wires into symbols that tell the Gospel story, and make a chenille wire chain that never ends.

Wonder What Stations (15-20 minutes)
Choose and move through the following activities:
- Try This: Move animal figurines on pool noodle "rafts" across a bin of water.
- Let's Play: Play a game like foosball on a tabletop.
- Create: Make and keep chenille wire creations.

Review Together (5 minutes)
Work together to create actions for words in the Bible verse, and give out Here & Home papers.

Supply List

- [ ] Bible bookmarked at Romans 10:9
- [ ] All Together Tasks labels (1 sheet for every 8 kids) (on page 8)
- [ ] Feelings Charts (1 for every 2 kids) (on page 9)
- [ ] crayons
- [ ] Here & Home papers (1 per child) (on page 151)

Wonder What Bin Contents

- [ ] pool noodle rings (pool noodles cut into 1-inch rings)
- [ ] jumbo or regular chenille wires
- [ ] dishpan
- [ ] water
- [ ] animal figurines
- [ ] jumbo craft sticks

The "Wonder What Bin"

This supply box is a key part of each All Together Sunday School lesson. This large container will store all the toys and supplies needed for the Play Together activities and Wonder What Stations. Each week, kids will "wonder what" is in store for them! Your Wonder What Bin could be a plastic storage bin, a treasure chest, a toy box, or any large container.

All Together Tasks

Supplies: All Together Tasks labels (1 sheet for every 8 kids)

As kids arrive, explain the special jobs and encourage each child to choose one to do today. Download and print the All Together Tasks labels or copy them from page 8, and let kids choose the jobs they want to do. It's okay if more than one child has the same job or if one child has a few jobs. Teachers can have another job, too!

Kids choose from the following jobs:

Ready Reader is ready and willing to read a Bible verse aloud.

Prayer Person prays aloud nice and loud so everyone can hear.

Happy Helpers jump at the chance to hand out supplies and clean up stuff.

Befrienders are on the lookout for those who need help and support.

Greeters say, "Hello and welcome!" to everyone as they arrive and "Have a good day!" to everyone as they leave.

Play Together (10-15 minutes)

Play with the kids, using their favorite toys and games to help introduce the Bible Point. Choose one or both activities.

Supplies:
- Wonder What Bin

Pool Noodle Path

Place pool noodle rings on the floor, creating a special path to get you from one side of the room to the other. See how fast you can move along the path without touching the floor.

Ask: What was it like to move across the room on such small circles?

Say: Imagine having a helper to guide and help you stay on the path—that could've helped a lot! Today we'll see that Jesus helps us when we can't help ourselves. We'll discover that Jesus saves us.

Simon Says

Play Simon Says. Take turns being "Simon" and leading the group.

Ask: Which action from the game did you like the best? Tell why.

Say: Today we'll hear a Bible verse that says Jesus is Lord. A "lord" is someone who is in charge of people—kind of like how "Simon" was in charge of coming up with actions. Today we'll see how our "Lord Jesus" is in charge and how Jesus saves us.

Talk Together (5 minutes)

| Kids talk in pairs about how they're feeling today. |

Say: Today we'll talk with God and hear what God has to say to us through words in the Bible. But first, let's talk together. How are you feeling today?

Form pairs, and give each pair a Feelings Chart and a crayon. Have partners each circle the face that reflects how they're feeling in this moment and then tell their partners why they chose that face. Be sure to find a partner, too, and participate with the kids as they chat.

Pray Together (5 minutes)

| Kids tell God how they're feeling and pray a prayer all together. |

Say: Thanks for talking with a friend! In the Bible, we read that we can pray and tell God anything. You'll see the words of that Bible verse printed on the Feelings Chart. If you'd like to read along, please do! Or you can simply listen as I read God's words.

Philippians 4:6 says, "Pray about everything. Tell God what you need, and thank him for all he has done."

Like we just talked with our friends, we can talk with God! Let's practice doing that now. We'll silently pray and tell God how we're feeling today. After our thinking prayer, we'll pray a special prayer all together.

Invite kids to get comfortable and close their eyes as they pray.

Pray: Dear God, we want to tell you how we feel today and why we feel that way. Pause for several moments of silent prayer. **Thanks for listening, God.**

Say: Now let's pray all together. We'll ask God to guide our time together today.

Watch and do what I do! After each sentence, I'll pause and we'll say the words "All together" together!

Pray: Dear God,

May we love [make the shape of a heart with your hands] **you and each other.** ("All together!")

May we listen [cup hand behind ear] **to you and each other.** ("All together!")

May we learn [point to brain] **about you and each other.** ("All together!")

May we laugh and have fun [high-five a friend] **with you and each other.** ("All together!")

Thanks for bringing us ("All together!") **today. Amen.**

Supplies:
- Feelings Charts (1 for every 2 kids)
- crayons

Download and print or make one copy of the Feelings Chart on page 9 for every two people. Instead of printing each week, consider placing the charts in plastic sheet protectors. Then kids can use dry-erase markers to mark how they're feeling. Simply clean off the markings for next week!

This prayer will set the tone for your time together each day. Each sentence helps to communicate the values in your classroom and invites God to help everyone do their part, no matter their age! When behavior challenges arise, you can guide kids back to this prayer to steer them toward loving behaviors.

📖 Bible Discovery (15 minutes)

Find and read a verse together, explore its Bible context, and talk about stories in the Bible that reinforce the main idea of the verse.

Supplies:
- Bible bookmarked at Romans 10:9
- Wonder What Bin

Find and read Romans 10:9.

Say: Let's hear a Bible verse that'll help us get to know God even better. Today we'll explore Romans 10:9.

The Bible is made up of Bible *books, chapters,* and *verses.* Chapters are longer and verses are shorter—usually about one sentence. So Romans is the book, "10" is the chapter, and "9" is the verse.

Invite the Ready Reader to read the verse from your marked Bible. Have everyone clap to thank the Ready Reader for reading.

A man named Paul wrote these words to some of the first Christians. Christians get their name from the second part of Jesus' name—Jesus Christ. People were first called Christians after Jesus went back to heaven. Christians believe Jesus' words and choose to follow him. Together, Christians are part of God's family.

Have kids turn to each other and say, "Hi, brother!" and "Hi, sister!"

It wasn't always that way. In the Old Testament of the Bible, we read about one man's family that God chose to be his special people. That man's name was Abraham, and his family was called the Israelites. They were named after one of Abraham's family members, whom God called Israel.

Ask: What's your family's last name?

Say: People's last names usually tell whose families they belong to. Give a few examples, using the kids' first and last names.

Through Jesus, God made a way for the Israelite family *and* all other families in the world part of God's family! Romans 10:9 tells what they have to do. Listen to it again:

"If you openly declare that Jesus is Lord and believe in your heart that God raised him from the dead, you will be saved" (Romans 10:9).

When you declare something, you say it! This verse declares that <u>Jesus saves us</u>. That's our Bible Point today. So every time you hear the words "Jesus saves us," give two thumbs up and say, "It's true!" To practice, repeat the Bible Point and response several times.

You may be wondering, "What does Jesus save from?" Well, those are good questions. Let's explore them together as we retell the story of Jesus— with these fuzzy wires!

146   All Together Sunday School Book 1

> **Make shapes with chenille wires to tell the Gospel story.**

Hold up the jumbo chenille wires. Have Happer Helpers give one to each person.

It all starts way back in the beginning when God created this wonderful world and a beautiful garden. God made everything perfect. Let's twist our fuzzy wires into something God created. It could be the sun, the moon, trees, flowers, anything! If you want to, you can pair up with a friend to make something bigger. Allow time. Encourage Befrienders to help younger kids when needed. After a few minutes, ask kids what they made.

God's creation was perfect. It all belongs to God—God's in charge of it all! God made people, too, and they got to walk with God and talk with God like close friends do. But then things changed. One wrong choice caused sin to ruin God's perfect world. Have everyone "mess up" and take apart their creations so they have misshapen wires.

Sin causes people to make wrong choices. Sin makes a mess of everything—including our hearts. God is perfect, and sin isn't. So when sin came into the world, it separated God from his creation. That hurts God's heart, and it hurts people to be separated from God. Have everyone shape their fuzzy wires into hearts.

Ask: When have you noticed sin in our world this week? Give a kid-friendly example. Perhaps you read about someone stealing something from a store, or you personally said something unkind to a family member.

Say: Sin may have made a mess, but God was still in charge. God loved the world so much that he gave his one and only Son, Jesus. The little Lord Jesus came to our world as a baby to save people from sin and how it could keep us away from God.

A star helped people find Jesus! Have kids work together to join their wires into a star shape. As they work, explain that "Lord" is another name for God. It's a name that reminds people that we belong to God and he's in charge. If you know it, sing the first verse of "Away in a Manger" as you make the star, emphasizing the line "little Lord Jesus."

The star showed the world that Jesus, the Lord, had arrived. The world still had sin and death in it, but God had come to save it!

When Jesus lived on earth, he showed people what God is like. He wasn't little anymore, but Jesus was still Lord! His actions showed that God is in charge. He healed people, helped people, and corrected people who thought they could fix sin themselves. Then it was time for Jesus to do what he came to do.

Jesus hadn't done anything wrong, but the people who didn't like Jesus had him arrested. The people who didn't like Jesus took him outside the town. There, they made fun of Jesus. They hurt him. They put his body on a wooden cross. After some time, Jesus died. It was very sad.

Jesus died to forgive the whole world's sin—including the wrong choices that you and I make sometimes—so our sin wouldn't keep us away from God.

Let's make one big cross shape with our fuzzy wires. A cross kind of looks like a lowercase letter "t." Allow time.

Any size of chenille wire will work for these activities, but jumbo chenille wires are just a little more special and fun!

Jesus died. But that wasn't the end of the story because <u>Jesus saves us</u>. *(It's true!)* **After Jesus died, one of his friends took Jesus' body down from the cross and wrapped it in a long sheet of cloth. Then he put it in a new tomb—that's kind of like a cave—that had been carved out of rock. Let's wrap up one of our hands in a fuzzy wire and pretend to place it in a cave, too. Watch and do this with me!** Lead kids to wrap a wire around one of their hands. Have them cover their wrapped hands with the other hand.

Jesus' body was placed in the tomb. Listen to what happened after that:

Read aloud Luke 24:1-3.

The stone had moved! Who's strong enough to do that? God, that's who! Sin may make a mess, but God is still in charge. An angel told Jesus' friends that God had raised Jesus from the dead! Have everyone carefully pull the wires off their hands, without straightening the spiral. Have kids place one end of the wire on the floor, press down, then let go and watch it spring to life! After a few moments, have them shape their wires into circles.

Make a chenille wire chain that never ends.

Now that we've remembered the story of Jesus, let's think again about Paul's message to Christians.

Read aloud Romans 10:9-10.

That's how people become Christians! It's how people can become part of God's family. No matter where they live, what their family name is, or even what wrong choices they've made, people can be saved from sin and death because <u>Jesus saves us</u>. *(It's true!)*

Sin and death still make our hearts hurt here on earth. But because of Jesus, there is no sin and no death in heaven. When Christians die, they get to go to heaven and be with Jesus! Life on earth stops, but their friendship with God keeps going forever. Someday all God's children will be together in heaven. Jesus will be Lord there, too. And we'll celebrate that we belong to Jesus!

Like a circle goes on forever, life as God's child will never end. Let's make some circles to show that. Link all the wire circles together to make a chain. Then secure the chain into a circle. If you have a smaller group, cut the wires in half and make smaller chain links.

Pray together.

Pray: Dear Jesus, we openly declare that you are Lord. You're in charge, and we are yours. May our hearts believe that God raised you from the dead. Thank you for saving us from sin and death and making a way for us to be your friends forever.

Ask the Prayer Person to pray a simple prayer or simply say "Amen!"

Wonder What Stations (15-20 minutes)

Kids will wonder and wander their way through these three free-flowing application activities. Young kids may gravitate toward some things while older kids are drawn to others.

Say: Let's keep exploring Romans 10:9 with the items in this Wonder What Bin. You'll have three choices—I wonder what you'll choose to do first!

Dramatically re-reveal what's inside the Wonder What Bin, and explain these three different options for kids to choose during a free-play time. After 15-20 minutes, tell kids you'll be cleaning up the Wonder What Stations in about a minute. Have Happy Helpers return supplies to the Wonder What Bin.

Supplies:
- Wonder What Bin

Imagine That

Imagine the dishpan with water is a big lake that the animals need to cross. Pretend pool noodle pieces are rafts. Place an animal figurine on a raft and gently push it so it reaches the other side of the water bin.

Ask: Tell about a time you saw a boat or were on a boat. What was it like?

Say: Like the animals couldn't cross the water on their own, we can't get rid of sin on our own. We can try and try to be good, but we'll still make wrong choices sometimes. Thankfully, Jesus saves us! *(It's true!)* We can let Jesus be in charge of helping us with sin so we can be forgiven and forever friends with God.

Let's Play

Play a game like foosball as you stand around a table. Form teams and assign goals. Gently hit a pool noodle ring with wooden craft sticks, trying to score. Choose two "goalies" to stand at the ends of the table and protect their teams' goals.

Say: In soccer or foosball, goalies make "saves" when they stop the other team from scoring and winning. Jesus saves us because he stops sin from being in charge of our lives. Jesus saves us. *(It's true!)*

Ask: Tell about a soccer game you saw or played in. What was it like to keep the other team from scoring?

As kids play, meander around the area, using these questions and comments to connect each activity to today's Bible verse and Bible Point.

Create

Make other cool things out of chenille wires to keep and take home. Ideas include animals, necklaces, or flowers.

Say: Those creations belong to you now. When we believe that Jesus is Lord, we belong to God! Jesus saves us. *(It's true!)* Jesus makes a way for us to be God's precious children.

Ask: What ways can you show that you're God's child today?

Lesson 12   149

Review Together (5 minutes)

> Work together to create actions for words in the Bible verse.

Supplies:
- Here & Home papers (1 per child)
- crayons

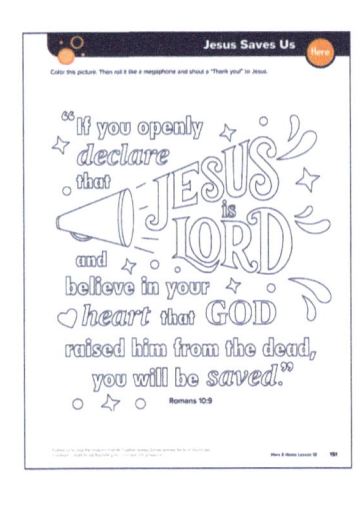

Say: Through Jesus, all people can become part of God's family. It doesn't matter what your first name is or what your last name is. When you believe in Jesus Christ and trust him to forgive your sin, you get Jesus' name: Christian!

Let's create some actions to do as we say Romans 10:9 all together. Rather than *me* telling you what to do, you kids can create the actions for us. You're in charge!

Invite kids to work together to make up actions for these words:

- openly declare
- Jesus is Lord
- believe in your heart
- raised from the dead
- you will be saved

Say Romans 10:9 together with actions:

"If you openly declare that Jesus is Lord and believe in your heart that God raised him from the dead, you will be saved."

<u>Jesus saves us</u>. *(It's true!)* **No matter what you do, friends, you are worth saving. Jesus loves you and forgives you.**

Take some time to affirm kids by name, saying: [Child's name], **Jesus loves and saves you.**

Here & Home

Give kids each the Here & Home paper on page 151. Invite them to color and complete the Bible verse page now, and point out the activity for them to lead their parents in at home.

150 All Together Sunday School Book 1

Jesus Saves Us

Here

Color this picture. Then roll it like a megaphone and shout a "Thank you!" to Jesus.

"If you openly *declare* that JESUS is LORD and *believe in your heart* that GOD raised him from the dead, you will be *saved*."

Romans 10:9

Home

Jesus Saves Us

"If you openly declare that Jesus is Lord and believe in your heart that God raised him from the dead, you will be saved" (Romans 10:9).

"Nobody's perfect." It's a short sentence with a lot of truth. Try as we might, humans won't always say the right thing or do the right thing. We're bound to do and say "wrong."

But there's hope. Notice what Paul doesn't write in Romans 10:9. He doesn't say, "If you try hard to be perfect and never do anything wrong, you will be saved." He doesn't even state, "If you're good most of the time and only mess up a little, you will be saved."

Instead, Paul points to Jesus. To paraphrase his words, "When we say we belong to Jesus and believe he beat sin and death, then we are saved."

Jesus saves. He saves us from sin and death and from the pressure we put on ourselves to be God's perfect children. Because of Jesus, we're part of God's family and we're dearly loved—mistakes and all.

Fun Fact

Did you know that in Romans 10, Paul rewrote words that Moses' said to the Israelites in Deuteronomy 30:14? Moses told the Israelites that this message from God was "on your lips and in your heart so that you can obey it." Paul's message about Jesus was said with mouths and believed in hearts, too!

Think & Talk

To "declare" means to say something. Declare something you liked about today.

Read & Do

Read Romans 10:9-10. Then declare to different family members that "Jesus is Lord." Be creative as you declare—you could say the words quietly, loudly, in a high pitch, in a low pitch...whatever you choose!

Say & Pray

Tell Jesus that he's in charge of your family's lives, and thank God for making a way for you to be part of his big family.

Lesson 12   153

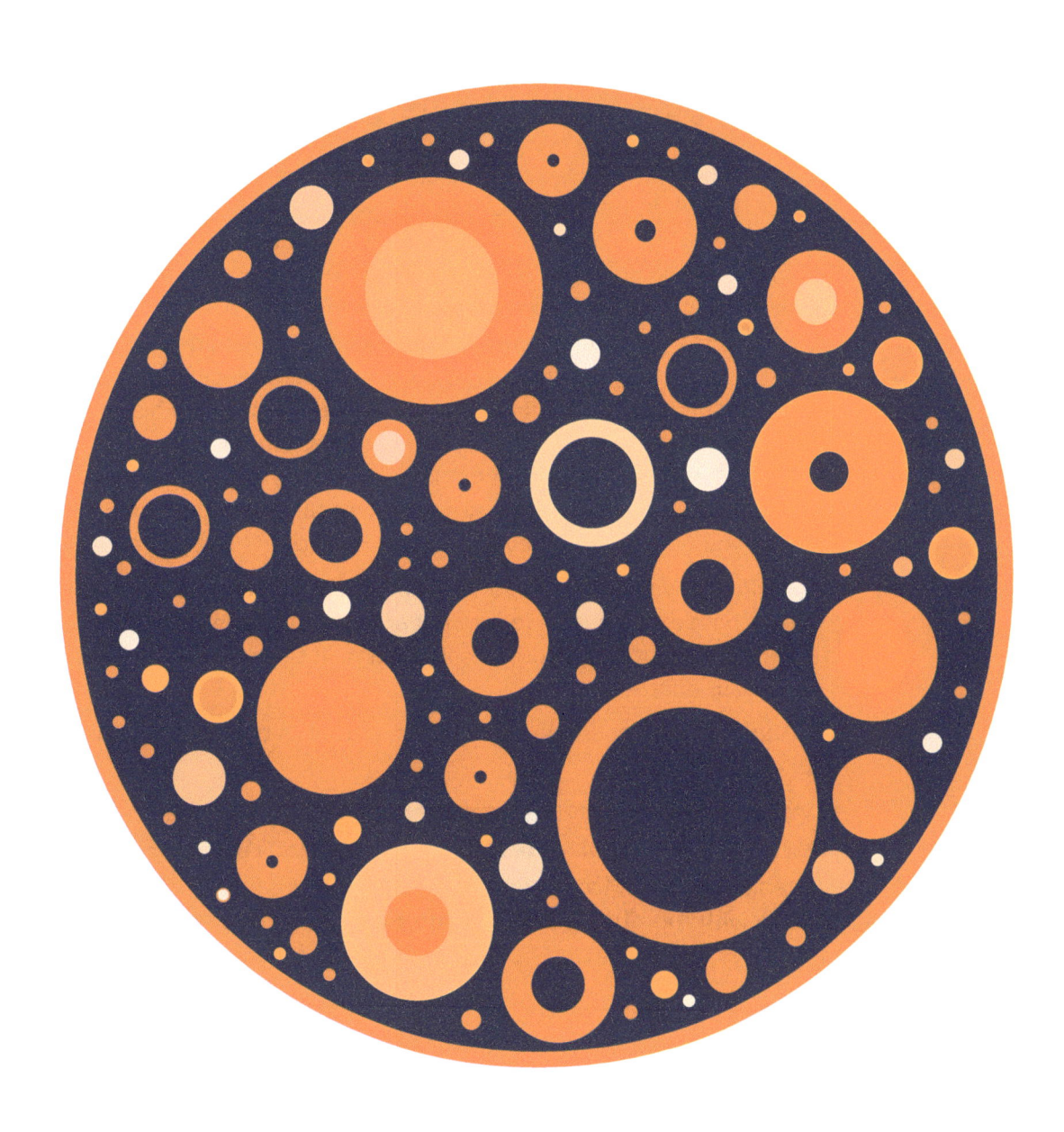

Lesson 13: God's Love Never Stops

"Love never gives up, never loses faith, is always hopeful, and endures through every circumstance" (1 Corinthians 13:7).

Discover 1 Corinthians 13:7

As humans, we're used to conditions. If we do this, then we expect that. If we don't do this, then we could not expect that. Maybe that's why it can be so hard to wrap our minds around God's unconditional love. God loves us, not because of anything we've done but because of who we are—his beloved children. What if we viewed each other like that, too?

Paul writes in 1 Corinthians 13, "Love never gives up, never loses faith, is always hopeful, and endures through every circumstance."

God is the source of extraordinary love. God has shown his children what true love looks like and helps us extend that love to each other.

The father in the parable of the lost son shows us what that never-ending love looks like, too. And with God's help, you can model that love to the children you teach today. May God love his children through you as you...

- Patiently wait for kids to sit inside the heart with you.
- Choose kind words to redirect activities and conversations.
- Put your hope in God, trusting that he'll speak to kids' hearts through your efforts.

God's love never stops. Enjoy being surrounded by that love as you teach today!

Fun Fact

A parable is a story that illustrates something true. Jesus often used parables to help people picture what God is like and what's most important to God.

PRAYER

Thank you, God, for never giving up on me. Your steady love has been with me during the ups and downs of this day. I'm so grateful. In Jesus' name, amen.

Lesson Overview

Bible Verse: 1 Corinthians 13:7 | **Bible Point:** God's love never stops. *(It's true!)* | **Bible Exploration:** Luke 15:11-32

Lesson-at-a-Glance

Play Together (10-15 minutes)
Play with hula hoops and/or have a staring contest.

Talk Together | Pray Together (10 minutes)
Talk about how you're feeling today, then pray and talk with God about it.

Bible Discovery (10-15 minutes)
Find and read 1 Corinthians 13:7 together, make a heart shape to sit inside, and explore the parable of the lost son—with action figures!

Wonder What Stations (15-20 minutes)
Choose and move through the following activities:
- Create: Design "Not-Valentine's Day" cards.
- Let's Play: Play a game like Hot Potato.
- Try This: Mix and drink lemonade.

Review Together (5 minutes)
Work together to create actions for words in the Bible verse, and give out Here & Home papers.

Supply List

- ☐ Bible bookmarked at 1 Corinthians 13:7 and Luke 15:11
- ☐ All Together Tasks labels (1 sheet for every 8 kids) (on page 8)
- ☐ Feelings Charts (1 for every 2 kids) (on page 9)
- ☐ crayons
- ☐ rope or yarn
- ☐ Here & Home papers (1 per child) (on page 163)
- ☐ colored pencils

Wonder What Bin Contents

- ☐ hula hoops
- ☐ 3 action figures
- ☐ music player
- ☐ upbeat music
- ☐ small bottles of water (1 per child)
- ☐ lemonade packets (1 for every 2 kids)
- ☐ half sheets of card stock (1 per child)
- ☐ heart stickers or heart stamps with washable ink pads
- ☐ washable markers

The "Wonder What Bin"

This supply box is a key part of each All Together Sunday School lesson. This large container will store all the toys and supplies needed for the Play Together activities and Wonder What Stations. Each week, kids will "wonder what" is in store for them! Your Wonder What Bin could be a plastic storage bin, a treasure chest, a toy box, or any large container.

Lesson 13 155

All Together Tasks

Supplies: All Together Tasks labels (1 sheet for every 8 kids)

As kids arrive, explain the special jobs and encourage each child to choose one to do today. Download and print the All Together Tasks labels or copy them from page 8, and let kids choose the jobs they want to do. It's okay if more than one child has the same job or if one child has a few jobs. Teachers can have another job, too!

Kids choose from the following jobs:

Ready Reader is ready and willing to read a Bible verse aloud.

Prayer Person prays aloud nice and loud so everyone can hear.

Happy Helpers jump at the chance to hand out supplies and clean up stuff.

Befrienders are on the lookout for those who need help and support.

Greeters say, "Hello and welcome!" to everyone as they arrive and "Have a good day!" to everyone as they leave.

Play Together (10-15 minutes)

Play with the kids, using their favorite toys and games to help introduce the Bible Point. Choose one or both activities.

Supplies:
- Wonder What Bin

Hula Hoop Spin

Play with hula hoops. Spin one on the floor, throw one in the air so it comes back to you, or try to make one go around and around your waist. Experiment and help each other try new things.

Ask: What's your favorite hula hoop move?

Say: A hula hoop's shape can remind us of God's love. Like a circle keeps going and going, God's love never stops.

Staring Contest

Have a staring contest with a friend. See who blinks first!

Say: We can't stare forever! Eventually our eyes need a break. Today we'll find out that God never needs a break from loving people. God's love never stops. It keeps going and going and going!

Ask: What game or show do you wish would never stop?

156 All Together Sunday School Book 1

Talk Together (5 minutes)

> Kids talk in pairs about how they're feeling today.

Say: Today we'll talk with God and hear what God has to say to us through words in the Bible. But first, let's talk together. How are you feeling today?

Form pairs, and give each pair a Feelings Chart and a crayon. Have partners each circle the face that reflects how they're feeling in this moment and then tell their partners why they chose that face. Be sure to find a partner, too, and participate with the kids as they chat.

Supplies:
- Feelings Charts (1 for every 2 kids)
- crayons

Download and print or make one copy of the Feelings Chart on page 9 for every two people. Instead of printing each week, consider placing the charts in plastic sheet protectors. Then kids can use dry-erase markers to mark how they're feeling. Simply clean off the markings for next week!

Pray Together (5 minutes)

> Kids tell God how they're feeling and pray a prayer all together.

Say: Thanks for talking with a friend! In the Bible, we read that we can pray and tell God anything. You'll see the words of that Bible verse printed on the Feelings Chart. If you'd like to read along, please do! Or you can simply listen as I read God's words.

Philippians 4:6 says, "Pray about everything. Tell God what you need, and thank him for all he has done."

Like we just talked with our friends, we can talk with God! Let's practice doing that now. We'll silently pray and tell God how we're feeling today. After our thinking prayer, we'll pray a special prayer all together.

Invite kids to get comfortable and close their eyes as they pray.

Pray: Dear God, we want to tell you how we feel today and why we feel that way. Pause for several moments of silent prayer. Thanks for listening, God.

Say: Now let's pray all together. We'll ask God to guide our time together today.

Watch and do what I do! After each sentence, I'll pause and we'll say the words "All together" together!

Pray: Dear God,

> **May we love** [make the shape of a heart with your hands] **you and each other.** ("All together!")
>
> **May we listen** [cup hand behind ear] **to you and each other.** ("All together!")
>
> **May we learn** [point to brain] **about you and each other.** ("All together!")
>
> **May we laugh and have fun** [high-five a friend] **with you and each other.** ("All together!")
>
> **Thanks for bringing us** ("All together!") **today. Amen.**

This prayer will set the tone for your time together each day. Each sentence helps to communicate the values in your classroom and invites God to help everyone do their part, no matter their age! When behavior challenges arise, you can guide kids back to this prayer to steer them toward loving behaviors.

Lesson 13 157

📖 Bible Discovery (15 minutes)

Find and read a verse together, explore its Bible context, and talk about stories in the Bible that reinforce the main idea of the verse.

Supplies:
- Bible bookmarked at 1 Corinthians 13:7 and Luke 15:11
- rope or yarn
- Wonder What Bin

Find and read 1 Corinthians 13:7.

Say: Let's hear a Bible verse that'll help us get to know God even better. Today we'll explore 1 Corinthians 13:7.

The Bible is made up of Bible *books, chapters,* and *verses.* Sometimes Bible books have the same name, so they're numbered. There are two books called "Corinthians." Today's verse is from the first one. Let's hear 1 Corinthians 13:7.

Invite the Ready Reader to read the verse from your marked Bible. Have everyone clap to thank the Ready Reader for reading.

When something "endures through every circumstance" it lasts all the time!

Ask: What does this verse tell us about God?

Say: This verse tells us that <u>God's love never stops</u>! That's our Bible Point today. So every time you hear the words "God's love never stops," give two thumbs up and say, "It's true!" To practice, repeat the Bible Point and response several times.

Make a heart shape to sit inside.

Love makes me think of hearts. Let's make a big heart on the floor that we can all sit inside. Clear furniture to create a large open area on the floor. Use rope or yarn to make a big heart shape on the floor. Then invite everyone to sit inside the heart and put a hula hoop in the center of the heart. Put the action figures inside the hula hoop.

When Jesus lived on earth, he taught people about what matters to God. After all, he *is* God, so he would know!

Use action figures to tell the story of the lost son.

One day, Jesus told some stories to help people understand God's never-ending love for all people. One story was about a father and his two sons. Let's imagine this hula hoop is their farm and these action figures are the father and the two sons. Together, decide which figure is the dad, which is the older son, and which is the younger son. Use card stock from the Wonder What Bin to show where the house, the barn, and the fields would be located.

Now that we have the setting and characters set, listen to the first part of Jesus' story.

📖 Read aloud Luke 15:11-12.

That wasn't a very kind request. It was actually rather rude. Asking for the money he'd typically get after his father's death was like saying, "Dad, I hope you die."

Ask: **If someone said that to you, how would you feel?**

Say: **The younger son's words and actions must have broken his father's heart and made him very sad.** Ask a child to hold up the "father" to make it shake with sobs and cry.

But still, the younger son took the money, packed his bags, and moved away from home. Have a child lift the younger son out of the hula hoop and hold him in the air away from the others and do a little dance. **Yippee!**

The son went wild and wasted all his money. Let's pretend we're on a wild roller coaster. On the count of three, everyone throw your hands in the air and let out a "Woo!" Demonstrate, then count to three and lead the kids in the wild ride several times.

Perhaps you've ridden a real roller coaster or seen people ride one. The wild ride seems pretty fun.

Ask: **Would you want to ride a wild roller coaster for the rest of your life? Why or why not?**

Say: **Wild, wacky adventures are fun for a while, but they often end up making you sick and tired! Well, the younger son was on a wild ride that cost him all his money. He couldn't buy food, and he was so hungry. Sometimes when we're hungry, our stomachs growl.** Have everyone hold their stomachs and make quiet growling noises.

The younger son got a farm job to make some money. He fed pigs. Let's imagine we're all pigs. Have a child hold the younger son in front of each person in the heart, as if feeding a hungry pig. Encourage pig snorts and noises.

The younger son was so hungry that even the pigs' food looked tasty. That's when he'd had enough. Have everyone shout, "That's enough!" **The younger son decided to go home and ask to be his father's servant. Not his son. After all, he'd been awful to his dad. But maybe he could be a servant and work for his dad.**

Have two kids hold the dad and younger son and be ready to act out the next part of the story as you read.

Read aloud Luke 15:20-24 with expression as kids move the figures to show the action.

Even after his son hurt his feelings, left, and wasted his money, the father's love never stopped. Point to the heart shape around you all. **Even when he left home, the father's love still surrounded the son.**

The older brother, however, wasn't so sure. He was mad that his dad was quick to forgive and welcome his little brother back. He didn't want to join the party. Instead, he sat and sulked. Have a child make the older brother figure lie facedown like he's having a pity party.

Remember when the father ran to meet his younger son? Well, now he went to find his older son, too. Have the child move the father over to the older son. Listen to what the father said.

📖 Read aloud Luke 15:31-32.

Point to the heart shape around you all. **Even when he stayed at home and had a fit, the father's love still surrounded the older son.**

Ask: How is the father's love like God's love for his children—including you and me?

Say: In Jesus' story, the father never stopped loving his sons. No matter where they went or what they did, they were surrounded by love. That's true for us, too. Jesus' story helps us see that our Father God never stops loving his children either. <u>God's love never stops</u>. *(It's true!)*

Explore 1 Corinthians again and pray together.

Much later, after Jesus went back to heaven, a church leader named Paul wrote to Christians who lived in a town called Corinth. Like bickering, jealous siblings in Jesus' story, they weren't loving each other and getting along so well. That's why Paul wrote them a letter to remind them what God's love is like. Let's read what he wrote again. I'll read a few more verses this time.

📖 Read aloud 1 Corinthians 13:4-7.

Humans don't always love like that. Instead we're impatient and unkind. We get jealous, like the older brother. We are boastful and proud. Sometimes, like the younger brother, we're pretty rude.

Even then, God's love never stops. Point to the heart you're sitting inside. **God's love surrounds us and isn't going anywhere. <u>God's love never stops</u>.** *(It's true!)* **And with God's help, we can love each other better, too.**

Let's show our love for each other with a group hug! Have everyone stand and put arms around each other for a group hug, if that's comfortable for everyone. **As we're here, surrounded by God's love for us, let's pray and thank God for his never-stopping love.**

Pray: Dear God, you never give up on us. Like the father in Jesus' story welcomed his son, no matter what we do or don't do, you always love us. Thank you. May we show your love to each other while we're all together today. And may we show your love to each person we meet this week.

Ask the Prayer Person to pray a simple prayer or simply say "Amen!"

160   All Together Sunday School Book 1

Wonder What Stations (15-20 minutes)

> Kids will wonder and wander their way through these three free-flowing application activities. Young kids may gravitate toward some things while older kids are drawn to others.

Say: Let's keep exploring 1 Corinthians 13:7 with the items in this Wonder What Bin. You'll have three choices—I wonder what you'll choose to do first!

Dramatically re-reveal what's inside the Wonder What Bin, and explain these three different options for kids to choose during a free-play time. After 15-20 minutes, tell kids you'll be cleaning up the Wonder What Stations in about a minute. Have Happy Helpers return supplies to the Wonder What Bin.

Supplies:
- Wonder What Bin

Create

Use card stock, washable markers, stickers, and/or stamps to make Valentine's Day cards—even if it's not Valentine's Day! Your creations will remind people of God's love for them each and every day!

Ask: Who will you give your card to? Why might that person need to remember God's never-stopping love?

Say: Let's celebrate God's never-stopping love more than one day a year. May your cards be a happy reminder that <u>God's love never stops</u>. *(It's true!)*

Let's Play

Sit in a circle. Play music as you pass an action figure around the circle. Have someone sporadically stop the music. The person holding the action figure when the music stops is out. Play until only one person remains—then play again!

Ask: How did you feel when you were out of the game?

Say: It's not very fun to have to stop playing a game when others keep going. But here's the good news: Since <u>God's love never stops</u> *(It's true!)***, we're never left out of receiving God's love.**

As kids play, meander around the area, using these questions and comments to connect each activity to today's Bible verse and Bible Point.

Try This!

Make lemonade! Open a small bottle of water and drink a little. Then add about half of a lemonade packet to the bottle. Close the lid, shake it up, then enjoy!

Ask: What if you wanted pure water again? Could you separate the lemonade? How is that like trying to separate us from God's love?

Say: Once it's mixed, nothing can separate the lemonade mix from the water. And nothing can separate people from God's love. What a sweet treat! <u>God's love never stops</u>. *(It's true!)*

Review Together (5 minutes)

> Work together to create actions for words in the Bible verse.

Supplies:
- Here & Home papers (1 per child)
- crayons

Say: God loved the world so much that he gave his only Son, Jesus. When he died on a cross and came back to life again, Jesus made a way for all people to become children of God. Through Jesus, we're part of God's family!

It's not always easy to love our brothers and sisters in God's family with love that's patient and kind and faithful and true. But God's love still surrounds us. God will help us love each other, and verses like 1 Corinthians 13:7 remind us what true love from God is like!

Let's create some actions to do as we say 1 Corinthians 13:7 all together. Rather than *me* telling you what to do, you kids can create the actions for us. You're in charge!

Invite kids to work together to make up actions for these words:

- Love
- never gives up
- never loses faith
- is always hopeful
- endures through every circumstance

Say 1 Corinthians 13:7 together with actions:

"Love never gives up, never loses faith, is always hopeful, and endures through every circumstance."

<u>God's love never stops.</u> *(It's true!)* **You are surrounded by God's love today and every day!**

Take some time to affirm kids by name, reminding them that God will always love them.

Here & Home

Give kids each the Here & Home paper on page 163. Invite them to color and complete the Bible verse page now, and point out the activity for them to lead their parents in at home.

162   All Together Sunday School Book 1

God's Love Never Stops

Here

Practice patience as you use colored pencils to color all the teeny-tiny shapes on this page.

"Love never gives up, never loses faith, is always hopeful, and endures through every circumstance."

1 Corinthians 13:7

Home

God's Love Never Stops

"Love never gives up, never loses faith, is always hopeful, and endures through every circumstance" (1 Corinthians 13:7).

God's love is unconditional. God loves you, not because of anything you've done but because of who you are—his beloved children. What if your family viewed each other like that, too?

Paul writes in 1 Corinthians 13, "Love never gives up, never loses faith, is always hopeful, and endures through every circumstance."

God is the source of extraordinary love. God has shown his children what true love looks like and helps us extend that love to each other.

The father in the parable of the lost son shows us what that never-ending love looks like, too. And with God's help, you can show that love to your family members today.

God's love never stops. Enjoy being surrounded by that love as you teach today!

Fun Fact

A parable is a story that illustrates something true. Jesus often used parables to help people picture what God is like and what's most important to God.

Think & Talk

Who showed you God's love today? What did that person do?

Read & Do

Read 1 Corinthians 13:4-7. Then make up a story—like a parable—that illustrates that kind of love from God.

Say & Pray

Think of someone who is a little hard to love. Pray for that person, and ask God to love that person through you.

Lesson 13

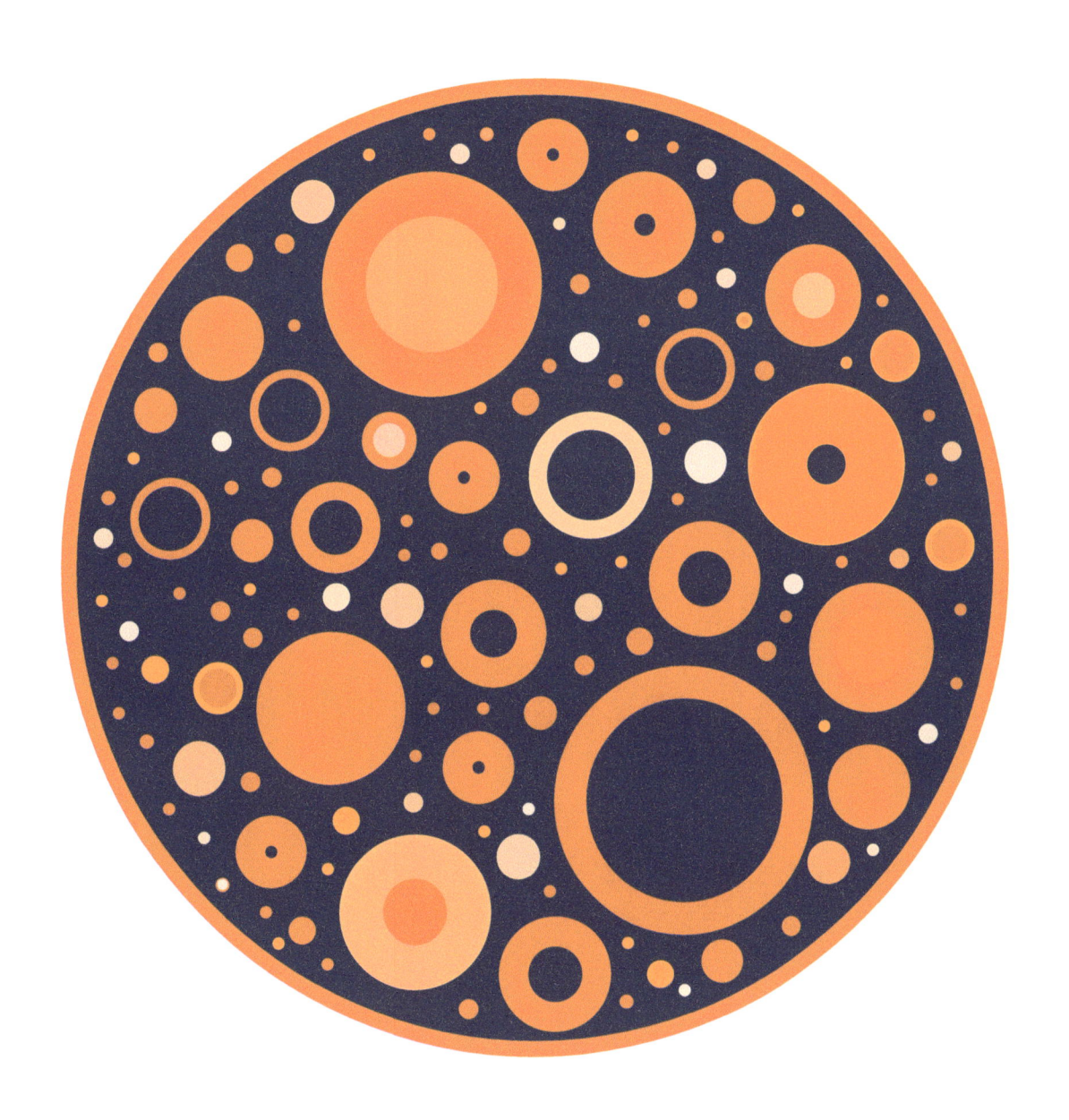

NOTES

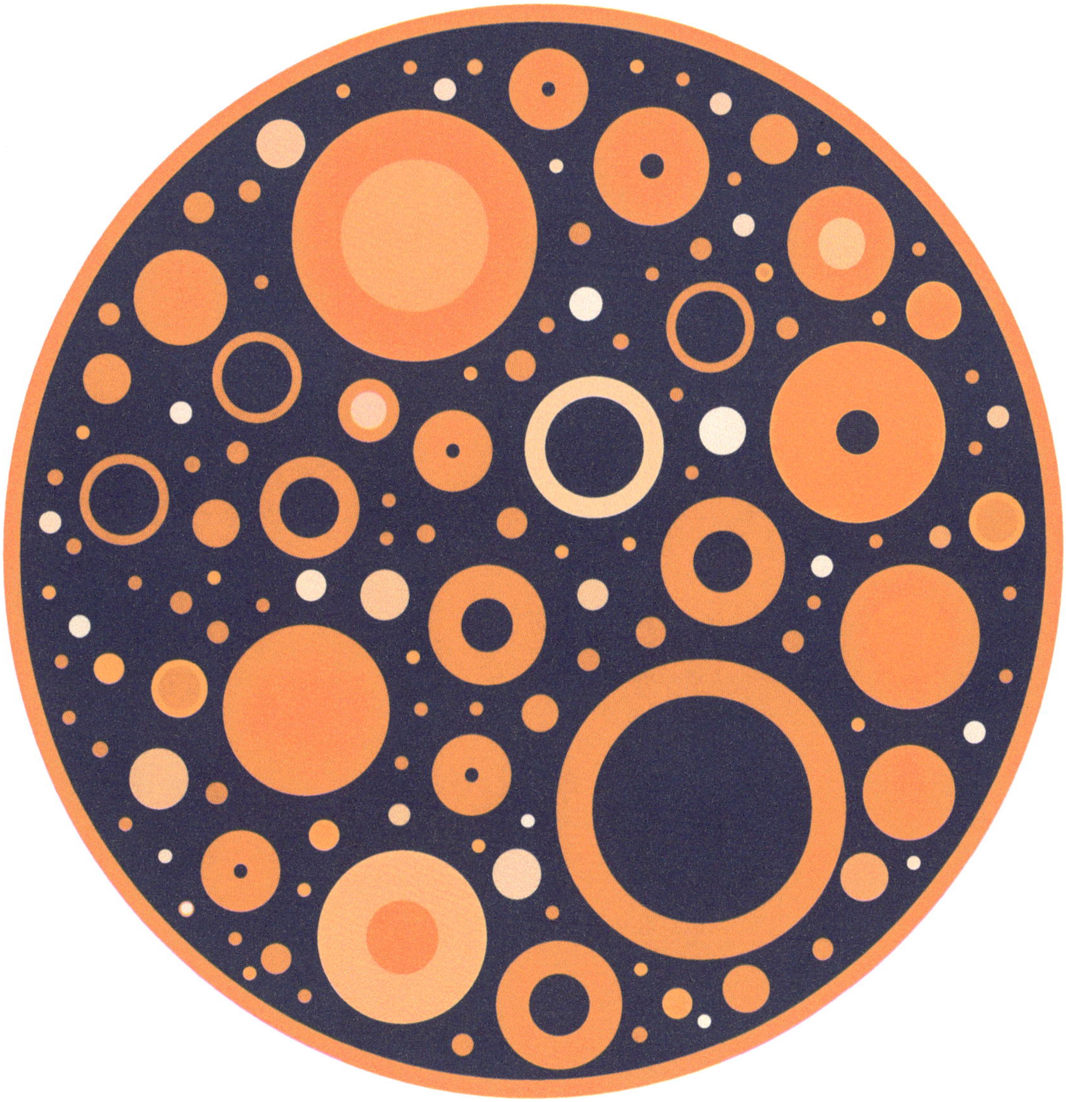

NOTES